I

Probably

Should

Have

Gone

to

Therapy

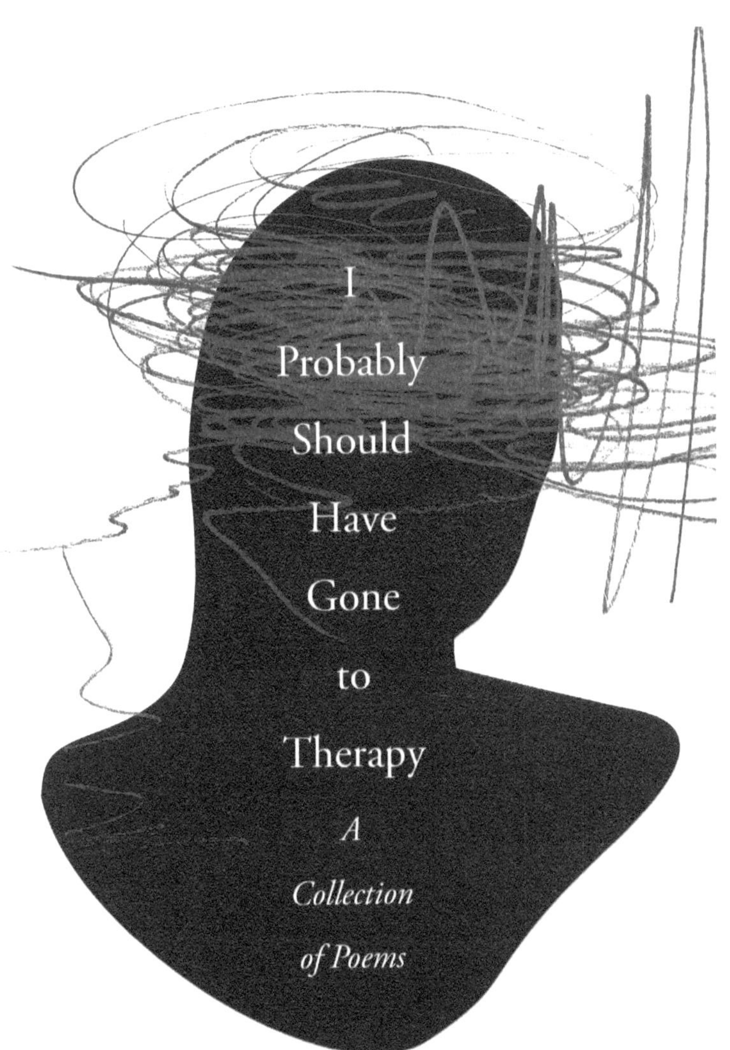

Darah DeWalt

Hardcover ISBN: 979-8-9952615-0-6
Paperback ISBN: 979-8-9952615-1-3
eBook ISBN: 979-8-9952615-2-0

First printing, 2026.

For younger Darah

We did it! We dreamed and we achieved.
I hope you're proud.

Keep staring at the stars, taking pictures of sunrises
& sunsets, and loving with your whole heart.

The only regret you'll have is not being your full self.
Shine bright baby.

Author's Note

This collection of poems explores a wide range of deeply personal experiences and emotions. *I Probably Should Have Gone to Therapy* incudes themes of grief, anxiety, depression, and suicidal thoughts. While these poems come from a place of reflection and hope to lead toward healing, these topics may be triggering to some readers. Know that you are not alone in how you feel. You are still here, still breathing, and still becoming. If you are struggling, know that help is available; you deserve support. There is no shame in asking for help.

Contents

Dear Reader,

Self-expression is meant to show how it feels to live, not give the facts. This is art, not a history lesson. You are about to take a trip through the depths of my brain, heart, and soul. Behind all the locked doors and towering walls is just a girl with a bunch of feelings; she's not too sure how to express them and not certain who to share them with, so she turned to a journal. Those emotions and those journal entries have turned into what you are holding right now. Raw feelings from moments throughout my life. Stories lived and told that I hope never die. People I love that I hope live forever. People that I've lost that I'll love forever. My hope is that you find yourself within the words. I hope by reading these poems, you can relate to them and know that you are not the only person who feels this way, that you are not alone, and that your feelings are valid. I hope that maybe you can learn something from my life experiences before you have to learn it yourself the hard way. I hope that if you're grieving, you can find some peace in my struggles with loss. Maybe you'll be encouraged to say those things you were scared to say. Maybe you'll be able to stand up to that voice in your head telling you lies about yourself and your worth.

Putting this project together was such a rollercoaster, but it brought me back to myself and opened my own eyes to what I needed to see. There's a quote from book called *Diary of a Tuscan Bookshop* by Alba Donati that reads, "Writing requires extreme care. It forces you to speak the darkness and, at the same time, see the beauty that blossoms within it." Writing has always been something that I do as an expression of my emotions and because I love putting pen to paper. For a while I ran away from that because I didn't want to deal with my emotions. It hurt too much, so I just stuffed them down and stopped writing. Eventually, I explored all that darkness, all the hidden crevasses of my mind, all the protected parts of my heart, and created this beautiful book of poetry that I had always dreamed of publishing.

So, while this book of poems is for you, dear reader, this book is also for "little me." She always dreamed of publishing a book, and she did. She always dreamed about sharing her words with the world, and she is. She has always dreamed of helping other people and making sure they know they are seen and loved, and her dream is coming true now. She's a little sensitive at times, very up and down, quick to love, quick to anger, slow to move on, and quite hard on herself. She is a part of me and this is for her too.

Be gentle with her and enjoy!

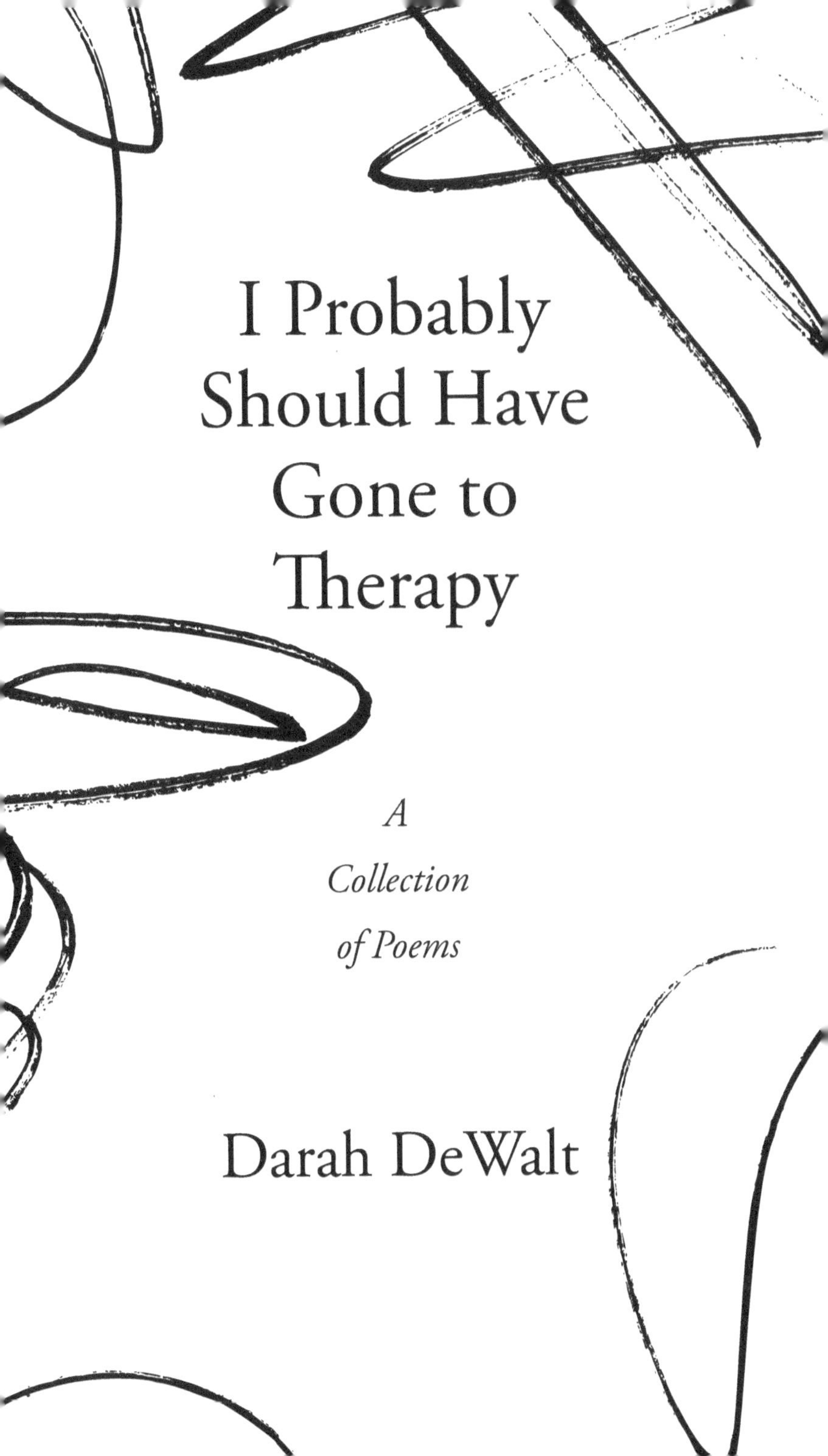

I Probably Should Have Gone to Therapy

A

Collection

of Poems

Darah DeWalt

Reflection

Growing up there were few people who were "cleared"
To read my work
       I trusted them
The teachers, mentors, and the secret keepers were en-
couraging
So why was I so hesitant to share?
       What was getting in my way?

I am familiar with her
I see her all the time
I can't escape her
I look at the mirror
       And stare at her dead in the eyes
You won't stop me anymore

The Me That Built These Pages

"*There is no other way to be.*
Aware but fearless."
— SHANIA TWAIN, *Not Just a Girl* Documentary

Where I'm From

Inspired by George Ella Lyon

I'm from black and white
I'm from the North and South
I'm from structure and silliness
I'm from intelligence and innocence
I'm from playsets and backyard pools
I'm from board games and books
I'm from babysitters and playdates
I'm from treetops and sandboxes
I'm from pencils and pens
I'm from playing outside till the streetlights come on
I'm from stars and grasses
I'm from the strength of my older brother
I'm from the weakness shown only to a few others
I'm from protection and peace, but chaos as well
I'm from my mom and dad whose love is unconditional
I'm from me which means I'm home

Home

Nothing else will ever be home

I love how you can walk outside in November
See the rainbow of autumn leaves
Contrasted with the bright Carolina blue sky
Wearing shorts and a T-shirt with no worries

I love the cool autumn evenings
When the moon is bright
The air is still warm enough for summer clothes
But when a breeze sneaks around the corner
You're glad to be sitting around a backyard bonfire

I crave the crisp burn the cold air makes
As you take a deep breath in winter
Or how the busy modern world goes silent and still
When snowflakes blanket suburban front lawns and rooftops
Only to be completely melted by noon

I love blistering hot summer days
When the pool deck cement burns your feet
And the smell of someone's grilled lunch
Diffuses throughout the neighborhood

Then mid-afternoon clouds begin to roll in
Foreshadowing a booming summer thunderstorm
    Flashes of lightning peeking through the blinds
    While waves of rain crash into the vinyl siding

I am Queen City, born and raised
With big dreams of traveling the world
But at the end of the day
I'm just a down home, southern, Carolina girl
And I always will be

Noche

I like to be up at night
With the moon and the stars
Enjoying the peace and quiet
Bathing in the darkness

Sometimes I don't want to go to sleep
      If I stay awake, tomorrow can't come
      If I stay awake, today will never be done
      If I stay awake, I can slow down and not have to run

Nothing can go wrong when I'm the only one awake
I can focus on every breath I take
It feels like I am stopping time
And anything I desire can be mine
No tears
No strain
No fears
No pain

It's just you
The moonlight
And the stars

At night

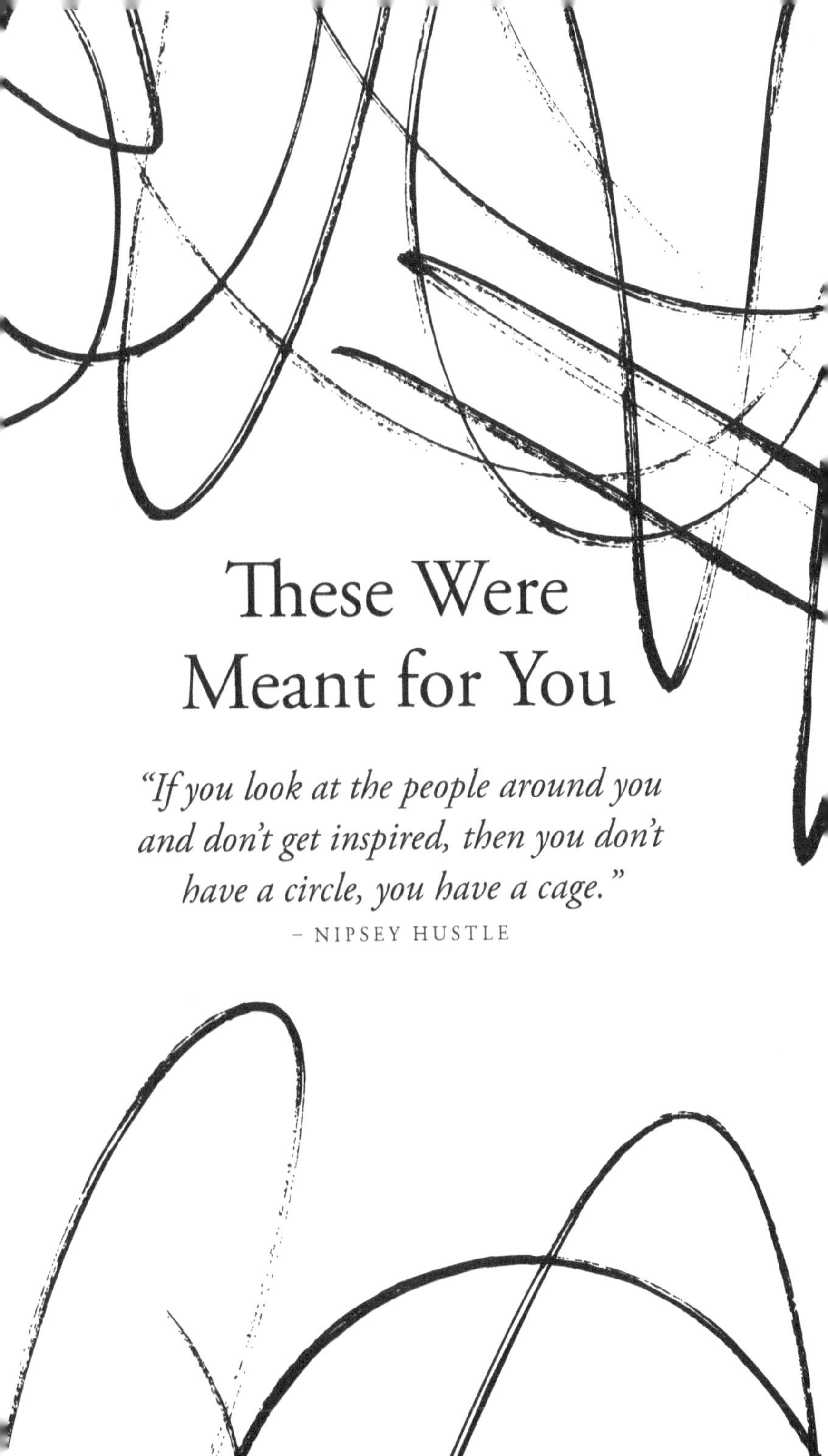

These Were Meant for You

"If you look at the people around you and don't get inspired, then you don't have a circle, you have a cage."

– NIPSEY HUSTLE

Starlight

For my friends

Life is a climb, but the view is great
Especially when you're out this late
Keep your eyes on the stars
And your feet on the ground
Because you can't see ahead
If you're always looking down

Friends are like stars, they come and go
But the ones that stay are the ones that glow
And no matter the distance, it's never goodbye
Because we are always under the same sky
Beneath the same sun, same clouds, same moon
So we can be reminded that we will reunite soon

The Counsel

For the girls

The three of us are very different
But the same in all the ways that matter
As a collective
One of us is gay as fuck
One of us is straight as fuck
One of us is single as fuck
Two mountain girls and a beach bum
Two North Carolina girls and a Tennessee gal
Three indecisive bitches
   But they are my ride or dies

Every time we're all in the same place
Watch out
We will be loud
We will be laughing
And once you get us started
There's no stopping us

I know I can go to them
   Any time
   About anything
   About anyone

And I take advantage of that.
They are my touchstones for perspective
In a world that changes too fast
They are what I hold on to
Three messy hearts
       And even messier minds
The three of us are different
But we never needed to be the same
We just needed each other

Keep Pounding
For Brian Blue

There was a man I came to know
And he was my number one fan
He believed in me from the start
Although he wasn't family
            He had the biggest of hearts
I'd look up in the stands
Knowing he'd be there
Screaming as loud as he could
You could always tell when Brian was in the building

Some people believe in ghosts
            Some do not
I choose to believe
Mine are guardian angels
And that he's always by my side
Cheering me on after every shot

There's no time to be blue
You're still with us but we miss you
And because of your belief in me was true
Instead of crashing
I flew
Thank you Brian Blue

Summertime in Waltsberg

For Grandpa Berg

It was a beautiful summer
The flowers had bloomed
The trees had blossomed
And the birds chirped with joy

But by the next day
It was gray
And I wanted summer to stay

All the leaves were dead
And all the animals went in
For a long winter's nap
They took the summer
Along with them

It was still and quiet
Like everything just froze
Like all the joy was taken—
In the summer all was good
But now it's sad and lonely

But what is this
I see with my little eye?
It's a big yellow kiss
Sitting in the clear blue sky

The Best Catch

Inspired by Derrick DeWalt and Walter Berg

I open my eyes and look out the window
I am instantly overwhelmed with color
   Blues, purples, and oranges began fill the sky
That's when I go to find Walt

We sit in the boat for the entire day
With nothing to eat but soggy wheat bread
Accompanied by ham, cheese, and lettuce
I will admit the conversation was better than the food

With our lines in the water
And Walt catching, unhooking, and recasting
   Far more times than I
He was the experienced one
He was catching the dinner I'd cook later

As the sun began to crawl beneath the horizon
And the stars made their evening debut
We drove back to the lake shore
It was too dark to see anyway
But I bet Walt would have stayed out there longer
   If I wasn't with him

Now I can't say I loved it
But I didn't hate it either
I may not have reeled in many fish
But I received something better that day—

A bond with my father-in-law

Family of Four

Inspired by my dad, Derrick DeWalt

It was always the four of us
Sometimes it was three—
   When Momma was at work
Sometimes five—
When one of us had a friend over
But at the end of every night
And the beginning of every day
We had our four.

Momma had three boys
And I was "that damn middle child"
   The talkative one
   The silly one
My older brother, Keith
Had a different father than
Me and my younger brother, Eddie
It didn't matter anyway
We were a family.

She worked all day long, for us
So we could have a home
So we could have food

We learned to cook
    Some better than others
So we could have nice clothes
And have our books for school
I am thankful for that.

My daddy, Willie-O, was around now and then
Usually drowning in booze
But he tried
He drove one of those big trucks
And took me for a ride once
I was young and didn't tell Momma
It ended up being a late night
We both got in trouble with her
Although, we got to spend some time together.

We all have our own families now
We all grew up and went separate ways
With Momma at the center
    With Momma in our hearts
We spend holidays together
And we have our clan of twelve
    Sometimes fourteen.

When cancer took my brother, our four
Was permanently three
It was sad, but I had to be strong
I'm the big brother now
And Momma needed me too.

I have my own four now
My wife, my son, my daughter
Sometimes two—
      When the kids are away at college
Sometimes three—
      When my son moved out.
But always four in my heart.

No matter the quantity
Fourteen, twelve
Two, eight
Four
Five
Six
We'll always be family.

Key to the Kingdom

For Great Grandpa Theodore

Days pass us by
As do the years
Some days we may cry
But we must not dwell on the tears.

Life isn't fair
And nobody said it would be
But we do what we dare
For all others to see.

"I got a key to the Kingdom
The world can't do me any harm"
He would say.
He would brighten everyone's day.

And everyone who knew him
Knows he wants us to be happy
Because the one thing he loved more than a hymn
Was his family.

I Love You, You Love Me

For Grandma Barbara

Stone, brick, small, and a little rough around the edges
A once gravel driveway, recently paved
There is a magnolia tree we used to climb
> We used it for hide and seek
> We used it for the goal line in front yard football
> We used to sit in it to take pictures
It grew with us

The woman who lives there
Is the sweetest, funniest woman I've ever met
A petite woman
> Short but so strong in every way
A smile brighter than the sun
Who gives the best hugs
> I never want to let her go

The scent of her freshly cooked food draws you to the kitchen
The taste requires you to go back for seconds
> Or thirds
> No matter how full you feel
The fridge stocked full of leftovers and Pepsi
You can hear the faint sounds of *Walker, Texas Ranger*

From the box set TV in her bedroom
Whenever it is time to leave
She'd stand on her front steps
No matter the weather
To smile and wave as we backed out of the driveway
We'd roll the windows down, honk the car horn, and wave back
Till neither of us could see the other

That is how I will always remember you
Never too sweet coffee
Jeopardy!
Chocolate attacks
Crossword puzzles
Smiling
Funny
Strong
Loving
And waving at us on your front porch
Behind the magnolia tree on Bancroft Street

Protect & Keep Safe

Inspired by my dad, Derrick DeWalt

Three boys and their mother
Lived in a house in Charlotte, North Carolina
Their fathers weren't around much
       Or at all
So, the eldest brother was left in charge
"Keith was my eldest brother"
"Responsible for me and my younger brother, Eddie"
"We challenged and combatted his every move and authority"
"He sacrificed his ego to keep us safe and out of trouble"
"He knew Mom expected him to be accountable for our well-being"
"If he harmed us or we got in trouble, *he* failed"
"His goal was not to disappoint Mom"
"Keith's role was to protect and keep safe"

Many years later
When the eldest brother lost his battle with cancer
It all finally made sense

"Today I am a better man, father, husband, brother, son,
and manager

Because of what I learned from my brother Keith"
"Don't take advantage of people because you are
stronger or bigger.

Just because you can."
"True strength is sometimes declining the physical fight
for the greater good"
"You don't hurt the people under your care"
"Your job is to protect and to keep safe"

The eldest knew they wouldn't understand in the mo-
ment
But one day, they would
"Now I do"

BOOP! That's a Marshmallow

For my mom, Judy DeWalt

We didn't always see eye to eye
Many times my feelings would get hurt
And I'd want to retaliate
		Sometimes I did
We spent so much time together
And there were times we **did not** get along
		Times I wanted to just be left alone
Looking back now, it hurts me to even think that

I just wanted freedom
I wanted to do what I wanted
I wanted to be on my own
I was envious of my brother who seemed limitless
		But it doesn't excuse how I acted
		Or take back the things I said

When I left home, I missed her
And when I returned, we learned each other's
boundaries

Things changed most when my grandma passed
        Her mom
I learned more about her childhood and where she's
from
I understood her more
It opened my eyes to the humanity of my parents

I'll never forget when they both grabbed my hands
        Tight
And cried in that Minnesota church pew
The tides turned
It was my turn to be the strong one
To care for and to comfort them
I realized they were just people too
        Figuring life out as they go
        Learning along the way
        Doing the best they can

So I held their hands tight right back
Handed them tissues

We think that parents shouldn't make mistakes
And should have all the answers
        We get frustrated when they don't

Now I don't want to imagine a day without my
mom
I will do anything to make up for the time I wasted
While expecting perfection from her
When, in reality, she was giving me all I needed
        Protection
        Lessons
        Memories
And most of all,
        Love

Lucky

For my parents

I may not be lucky enough
For my kids to know my parents
  The way I knew my grandparents

I may not be lucky enough
To have my mom around
  When I have my first kid
  When they ask a question that I don't know the
answer to

I may not be lucky enough
To have my dad walk me down the aisle
  To have a father-daughter dance at my wedding

But I am lucky enough to be raised by them
I am lucky enough to have them as a model
I am lucky enough to be able to call them friends now
I am lucky enough to enjoy their company
I am lucky enough to have memories to hold on to
  When I can't hold them anymore

And my future family will be so grateful
That I was lucky enough to be my parents' daughter

Ode to Camp Eagle Rock

For all my fellow Eagle Rockers: past, present, and future.
For you to reminisce with me.

In this little world of ours
We leave everything at the gate
We love our twenty-two acres of land
We climb, fish, draw, swim, and paint
We have friends that are hotter than hot
We slip and we slide
We sing songs even when the sun's too bright
We say "Hey" to burritos
We say "Good Morning" to birdies
We watch Tarzan swing from rubber bands
We all want to be a pizza man
We build each other up as a team
We wage wars with water balloons and spirit chal-
lenges
We play gaga ball till our knuckles bleed
We sing and dance in the rain
We lose our voices
     And are proud if it
We have spirit
We Boomerang

35

We run and do not grow weary
We walk and are not faint
We grow up and grow together
We are CER
We are Family

The tradition will always continue

Thank You, I'm Sorry, and I Love You

Thank you to the old coach who brought me here
    You gave me the opportunity to play in college
    You gave me the means to get a higher education
    You taught me how to persevere through poor circumstances
    You taught me that the way you treat people matters
    You taught me to appreciate finishing strong

Thank you to my teammates throughout the years
    We went through so much
    You taught me to have confidence in myself
    You restored my faith in people's ability to be there for me
    You helped me through the worst circumstances
    You encouraged me not to give up
    You supported me
    You helped me become a leader
    You made me laugh, cry, smile, and yell
    You helped me accomplish goals I had only dreamed of
    You helped me recover and heal
    You hold a special place in my heart

Thank you to my roommate of three years
    We first bonded via *American Ninja Warrior*
    You made me smile on the worst days
    We had so many fun adventures

We endured so much together and made it through
We became friends
We survived the year we were forced to not be roommates
We started and ended all the prank wars
I'll probably miss you most of all

Thank you to my English professors
You worked with me through all my injuries and illnesses
You pushed me to perform my best in the classroom
You helped me grow as a person as well as academically
You had faith in me when I didn't even have faith in myself
You listened
You taught
You supported me in every way, shape, and form.
You did much more than you were required to do as professors

Thank you to my athletic trainers
I spent more time with you all than I ever thought I would
You helped me through some of the most painful and scary
events I've experienced
You showed me kindness
You taught me so much
You supported me on and off the court
I'm honored to call you all friends

We had many conversations, vent sessions, and fun times
You went through everything with me, which I am both
thankful for and sorry for

Thank you to my current coaches
    You pushed me out of my comfort zone
    You helped me attain all the goals I set
    You celebrated my achievements with me
    You built a new foundation
    You showed up when we needed you most
    You were, are, and will always be in our corner, and made
    sure we knew that.

Thank you to the campus of Montreat College
    We had a rocky start and I was challenged by a friend to
    find the beauty
    And I did
    For showing me God's creativity
    For reminding me that I am a part of something bigger
    For bringing all the people previously mentioned into a
    common place to impact my life
    For preparing me to be launched into the world

Thank you to my friends back home
    You saved me when I needed to be saved
    You wiped my tears metaphorically and literally
    You stood by my side and let me lean on you
    You made sure I knew I was loved, even when I didn't feel

like it
You came to my games and cheered me on
You checked on me
You sent me letters
You visited me, making sure I didn't feel alone
You listened to me talk about all my struggles
You had my back about issues you weren't even involved in
You'll always have me, just like I hope to always have you

Thank you to my parents
  At least one of you were at every game, both home and
  away
  You supported me like no other and always have
  You paid for two surgeries, an ambulance ride, and an
  emergency room visit
  You allowed me to grow as a person, player, writer, stu-
  dent, and leader
  You made sacrifices
  You taught me all I know
  You stood by me
  You went to bat for me when I needed you
  You did more than I can ever describe or repay you for

Thank you to my brother
  You made me laugh
  You kept me sane
  You listened to my problems
  You took my calls at all times of the day

You made me realize how lucky I was
You gave me perspective
You're my partner in crime
You're my best friend
You're my co-pilot
You're in my heart forever and ever

Last but not least, thank you to basketball
    You were my first love
    You've been a part of my life since I was five years old
    You've brought some of my best friends into my life
    You were there when I was stressed
    You were there when I was mad
    You were there when I was happy
    You were there when I was sad
    You were there even when I wasn't there
    You'll never fully leave me
    I blamed you for my struggles and for that I am sorry
    I don't hate you
    I didn't like the way people were changing the game
    And although I am retired and creating some distance
    It is not out of an ill place, but out of growth
    It was unfair for me to treat you with malice
    When all you've done is be there for me
    You allowed me to go to college
    You introduced me to some of my mentors
    You made me a leader
    You made me stronger

So forget what I said in the past
While projecting my unhappiness
Forgive me for how poorly I've spoken of you
You're one of the best things in my life, no matter what
I've said, done, or not done
Though my days of playing are over, our relationship is
nowhere near finished
I love you

Just Us

For my friends

When we stand there with each other
Everything and everyone else melts away
>No matter where we are
>No concern for who is around
>No awareness of what time it is
>No regard for what's happening around us
It is just us.

That's all that matters
And I love that.

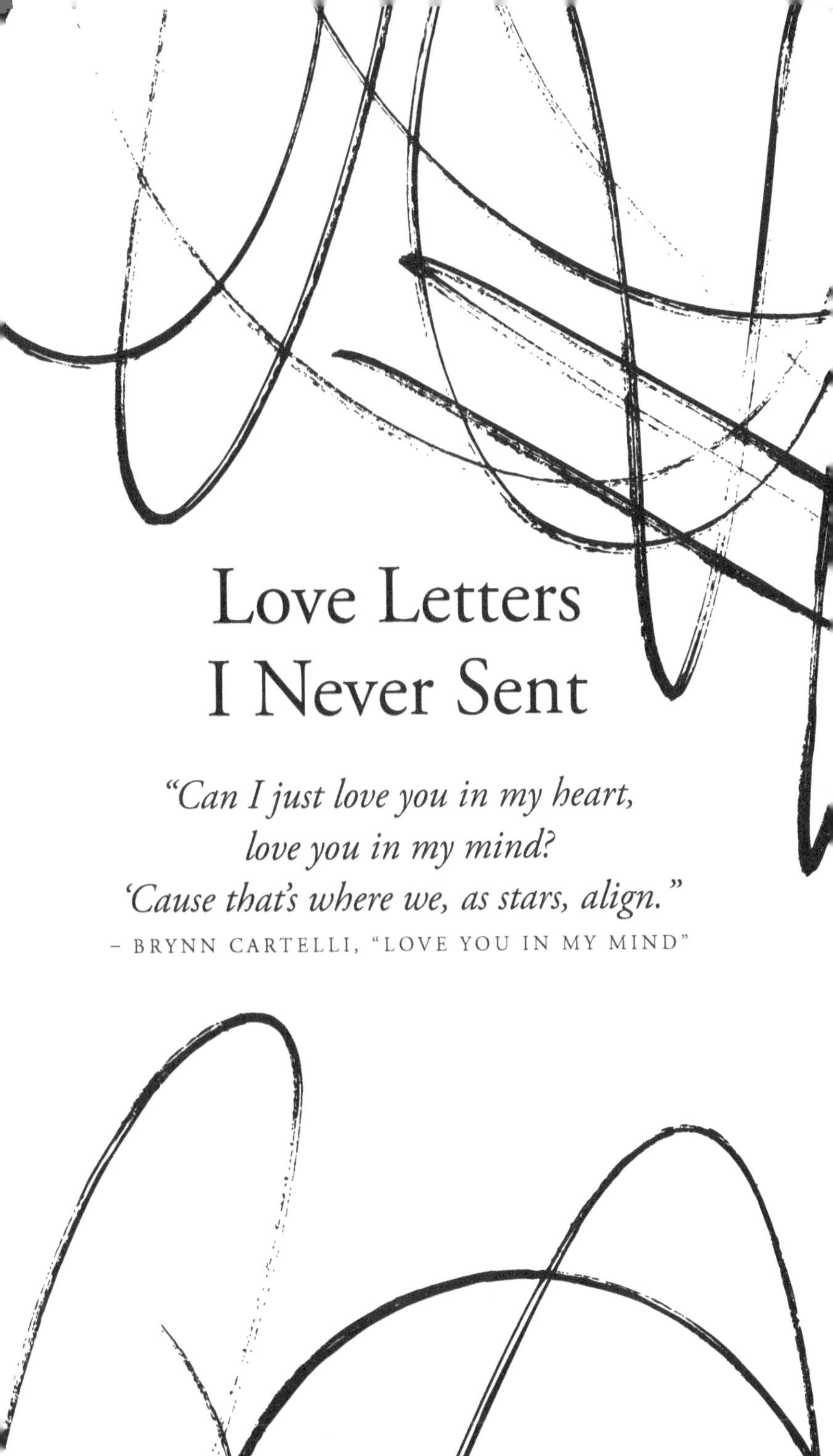

Love Letters
I Never Sent

"Can I just love you in my heart,
love you in my mind?
'Cause that's where we, as stars, align."
– BRYNN CARTELLI, "LOVE YOU IN MY MIND"

Lost In Love

Lost in thought
Lost in the instance
Lost in your eyes
Lost in the distance
Lost out of sight
Lost in existence

This is what I was scared of
I'm lost in love

A Ponder of Love

If you're asking if I need you
> The answer is forever
If you're asking if I'll leave you
> The answer is never
If you're asking what I value
> The answer is you
If you're asking if I love you
> The answer is I do

If you're asking how I feel about you
> The answer is a dream come true
If you're asking me how much I love you
> The answer is with my heart and soul too
If you're asking me how long I've loved you
> The answer is from the second I saw you

Little Did You Know

I don't want you to be the one that got away
But I don't want to waste my life trying to make you stay
You're supposed to be with me is what I'm believing
Although it looks like love, I guess looks can be deceiving

You should know I cry
Because I know you won't be mine
You should know
I am still praying that the stars will align
You should know
For you, I'll always fight
Even if it's wrong, because it feels right

I bet you didn't know
You're why I keep holding on
I bet you didn't know
You make me strong
I bet you didn't know all I want to do
Is be with you

I wish you knew your smile makes me melt
I wish you knew exactly how I felt

Little did you know
I loved you

Fairytale of You and Me

Wouldn't it be great to know what it feels like
To have a prince come and rescue you
Like the ones in the stories do
Slay the dragon and set me free
I want to be the one you need
I want to live the fairy tale of you and me

I can see a shooting star
And I wish to know where you are
Because you light up my whole night
You shine so bright
So won't you come and find me tonight?

Finally I am living free
With my prince that came to be with me
At last fate has intervened
Just like I've always dreamed

The two of us agreed
This is all we need
And it turns out this is just the beginning
Of "You and Me"

Destiny

Me and you have known each other for a while
We know how to make each other smile
Since I met you, you've been in my heart
I've known I needed you from the start

When we get into a fight
I can never sleep through the night
I stare through the window at the moon and stars
Knowing you see them too, wherever you are
We bring the hostility to a halt
Because we realize life's too short to worry about fault

And now it's time for the world to see
How you've changed me
      Brought light to my eyes
The love we share never dies
To spend forever with you, I'd go to extremes
Because I can't just love you in my dreams

Astronomical Love

Do you see all the stars in the night sky
That's how I see the sparkle in your eye
When you touch me, my heart races like a shooting star
I love you just the way you are

If your eyes were the stars and the moon was your smile
I'd look up at your face and stare for a while
And when those clouds of gray cover your face
I'll be the sun to push those clouds away

You're the flowers and trees
Rain, summer heat, and winter breeze
You're everything I need

You're the sun
        The brightest star in the sky
You're my universe.
You're my world
        The stars don't compare
        The moon doesn't compare
        The sun doesn't compare
You are my love.

One of a Kind

We met a few years back
Man I wish we could flash back
I guess it was just summer love
Hanging out with the moon above
Smiling and laughing with our friends
Too bad it all had to end
I was crazy for you, and it got in our way

I thought when I met you, I knew who you were
Nothing stood in our way
But those times are now a blur
You used to be kind, but one day that changed
Our relationship became estranged
And when you left, I almost lost my mind
You were everything to me—
One of a kind

If Only

We had that one night
But she's the love of your life
To steal your love
Wouldn't be something I'm proud of
Since I want you to be happy
With or without me

If only I could look into your eyes
If only I had your lips to kiss
If only we didn't have to say goodbye
If only I had no one to miss

Behind my smile is a hurting heart
Behind my laugh, I'm falling apart
If you look at me closely
You'll see the girl I am
Isn't me

If you could see into my soul
You'd see what my heart holds
Just the sound of your name
Can bring so much pain

If only you knew the truth
That I love you
If only I had the chance
Not just a hidden glance
If only I had a time
A time where you were mine
I'd rather see you with her
Than lovesick with me
I know we could be happy
If only, if only

Young & Reckless

We left the party early and hopped into your car
Went for a drive as it was getting dark
Blasted your music all through the town
We didn't care, we were just along for the ride
I thought to myself it doesn't get better than this
No it doesn't get better than this

Cruising with the windows down on the back roads
Your arm around me as we drove
The top was open so we could see the stars
As long as I'm with you, I don't care where we are
You take me to heaven, up past the clouds
You have my heart and it's beating loud

You pulled into a field and looked at me
Said there was no place you'd rather be
I felt your warm, soft lips connect with mine
And I felt as if I could freeze time
I looked into your moonlit eyes
And said let's be young and reckless for the rest of
our lives

As long as the sky is blue
I want to be young and reckless with you

All the Things
I Never Said

*"The words left unsaid hang heavier
than those we ever dared to speak."*
– WIDELY ATTRIBUTED TO EMILY DICKINSON

But I Won't

Could I have feelings for you?
> The smile
> The eyes
> The compassion
> The silliness
> The charisma
> The concern
> The comfort
Of course I could,
Everything feels so natural.

Even if I did, would I say it out loud?
No.
I wouldn't change a thing.
Because if we weren't able to be friends anymore
> If the jokes ran dry
> If the conversations faded
Then the fire would die
And I would not survive.

Could I be infatuated with the idea of you?
      The idea of us
      How life could be?
Absolutely.
But would I risk it all on an idea?
      I can't
      I won't
You deserve so much better
      So much more
Than to be loved by someone
Who's only in love with the idea of you.

If I'm being honest
You work my nerves day in and day out
You know how to grind my gears
You know exactly which buttons to push
      For the reaction you want
You can be like nails on a chalkboard
But you're still my favorite face to find in a crowded
room.

If I am being honest
I could love you
And I could do it forever.
But I would never allow myself to admit that
        Never actually let myself do that
And for the sake of being honest
It's because I'm scared
And that's why the one who gets to be claimed by you
        The one you get to claim in return
Is the luckiest person in the world
But that person will not
Be me.

Boundaries

I want to say everything
I've stopped myself from saying in the past
But would it be too much?

I want to wrap you up in my arms
And never let you go
But would I hold on too tight?

I want to see the smile on your face when the door opens
But would that be too much to ask?

I want to scream at you
For all the times I needed you and you weren't there
But would that matter to you?
Would it even make me feel better?

I want to scream at myself
For every time I needed someone
And stopped myself from reaching out
But would you answer if I did?
Would it make a difference if you answered?

Under normal circumstances, I could tell you how I feel
       I could be honest
I can say it out loud when no one's around
But if I had to say it to you
I wouldn't make a sound
I spend all my time with made up people
       With a pen and paper
       With music on a speaker
       With a glass of something strong

I feel like any word I say
Could push you even further away
The distance between us is all I know
And I'm afraid all it can do is grow

Silent I Stay

I needed a friend
I needed to talk about what was weighing me down
But silent I stayed

I needed support
I needed a shoulder to cry on
But silent I stayed

I needed to feel safe
I needed to feel seen
But silent I stayed

I needed to feel like I mattered
I needed to feel like I belong
But silent I stayed

I needed to be reminded what joy was
I needed someone to prove that love can still exist
But silent I stayed

I needed to stand up for myself
So I learned to speak up

I said I needed to be the one who is chosen
I said I needed someone to rely on
I asked for help
Yet it seemed as if I were silent again
      And silent you stayed

So now I will choose to be
Silent
Forevermore

Validation

Arguing is not communication
       Both people's minds are already made up at
that point
We need to really listen to each other
Rather than listening for the sake of a response
       A reply
       Or retaliation
That's effective communication

Sometimes you may not like what I have to say
And I don't like having to say it

If you don't respect me enough
       To appreciate my honesty
If you don't care enough to try to understand
       Why I'm feeling this way
That is the problem.
Not my words.

Some Wishes Come True

I know you love me
But that doesn't validate the way you treat me
I'd wait through your phases
I just hoped I wasn't one of them
You talk to me when it's convenient for you
Regardless of my needs
          And that's not right
You can't just fill my cup
When you want to drink from it

You said you didn't want or need help
You said not to worry about you
I guess you got your wish
It makes no sense to fight for someone
Who doesn't want to be fought for
You're free to do whatever the hell you want
          As if you weren't doing that before

I'm stepping back
You've successfully pushed me away
Congratulations

Silence

You ghosted me
Then you made me feel like it was my fault.
You can't push me away,
Then wonder where I went.

You made me feel like I did something wrong
      And maybe I did.
I wouldn't know,
      How could I?

Love is a Verb

The person I created in my head was my best friend
She showed up unannounced
      Especially when I had a shitty day
She promised to be my number one fan
She drove me crazy
      We had plenty of arguments
      But soon after, we'd be laughing again
It was all a fantasy.

Then all of a sudden
      But maybe only suddenly to me
It all got fucked up.

I thought I had done something wrong
So I did everything I could think of to try to save it
      Random coffee deliveries at work
      Birthday surprises
      Came over every time you asked
Then you asked for space
I was just trying to help
And you pushed me away.
It hurt.

Then I realized
We had two different ideas of what our friendship was
      You were my best friend
      But to you, I was just a person
I was fighting for a friendship that wasn't real.

We used to kid about one-sided relationships
I never thought I'd be the butt of the joke
"It's not one-sided"
Isn't it?
Your issues always trumped mine
      I was just emotional or sensitive
      I overreact and you have real pain.

How many times did I drop everything for you when
you needed me?
How many times did you ignore me when I said I
needed you?
How many times did you invalidate my feelings
when I shared?
We were never best friends
      You were mine
      But I was never yours.
You don't treat your best friends the way you treated
me

I deserve better
I was a great friend
But you'll realize that
Once you've lost me.

Actions speak louder than words
To love is a verb
It takes action, not just words
I hope that someday you'll understand that
Or else life is just going to get harder
Goodbye, my friend.

"I'll make this right."
        I won't hold my breath.

Where Are You?

The first time we met I thought I knew
What we were supposed to be
We clicked instantly
There were so many things yet to come
But what sucks is all the memories
       All the could be's
Are drowned out by the should have been

Where were you?
You didn't make it to any of the milestones
I reached in my life
And I would have settled if you showed up once
I tried to always be there for you
You never needed to ask
And all you've done is push me away
When you told me we'd be friends forever
My soul said to believe you
       So I did
Now I look like a fool

I opened up
I told you everything
About the people who hurt me most
       Then you did it to me
My biggest fears
       You made them come true

You always said
"I don't know what to say to help"
"I can't say anything to make you feel better"
        But all I wanted was for you to try
Just being there
        Even if it were in silence
Would have helped
If you really knew me, you'd know that
Maybe you didn't know me
        Didn't care
That's the only way I can make sense of this

Iceberg

Our friendship seemed like one thing at the start
But looking back it was different
Under the surface
There was a catch I couldn't see

I let you in
        But I shouldn't have
I built myself up
        But you broke me down
I needed you
        But you were busy
I told you everything
        But you didn't listen
I'd drop everything for you
        But you wouldn't do the same
You were a part of all of my dreams for the future
        But they are nightmares now
I talked about you constantly
        But I can't even say your name anymore

I grew up

But you stayed the same
I still love you
But I wish I didn't
I'm trying to remember the good times
But they don't cancel out the bad
I'm waiting
But you've moved on
Our friendship was everything to me
But it was just another relationship to you

Dear Former Soul Sister

To the one I don't talk to
      And the one I can barely talk about

Time keeps rolling on
If I'm busy, it can't get to me
      But when I'm alone
The pain comes like a freight train

I should not miss you
After all it was my decision
      So it shouldn't hurt, right?

I have every right to blame you
      But I don't
You broke my trust
      Made me question everything
      Everyone

At first all I felt was anger
I was so happy and trusting before you
Now I'm closed off all the time
It was the first time someone I trusted
      Completely
Broke that trust
And my heart

Some days I think I want an explanation
Other days, I just want to cry and scream at you
        Neither would help.

I've moved on
I have great friends now
        That I can trust
The pain may have subsided
        But the scar will never go away
I am guarded now
And I don't think that will ever change

I wish more than anything I could forget you
        As it seems you forgot me
I wish I could believe people when they say
        "You can trust me"
Instead of that being my new red flag

When people ask what happened between us
        And I start to tell them
My entire body shivers
I feel nauseous
My words are shaky
Tears fall

I don't regret our friendship
But if I could wish you out of my head
I'd do it in a heartbeat

I don't wish you the best
I hope you miss me too
I hope everything comes flooding back
        When you hear that stupid song
That may sound harsh
But the truth can hurt
        Sometimes more than lying
You taught me that

Truth and Lies

When I found out you were lying to me
I gave you a chance to come clean
          All would be forgiven
And you said nothing.

Lying about the important things
Tells me you don't trust me with the facts
          A problem of its own.
I'd rather be hurt by the truth
Than blindsided by it because of a lie.

Please remember this for the future.
If you find yourself in a lie
And someone throws you a bone
          Gives you an out
Fucking take it.

So the next time you don't think I like your boyfriend
          Or you'd rather hang out with someone else
          Or think I can't be emotional while sober
          Or don't want me around
          Or forgot about the plans
          Or don't care about what I'm saying
Be honest.
Give me a chance to know the truth
Before you hurt me with a lie.

Two Sides

You'll probably make me
The villain to your story
And if that's what you need to do
Go ahead

I missed you
I love you
The space never got easier
I cried about it
       More than I care to admit
I was shattered
And I put the pieces back together myself
       But I put them back different

So be my guest
Make me the villain
       Most days I'm my own villain too
But keep in mind
I'm only your villain
Because it was the title I was given
By you

Hurt

I just want you to know
      Even if it wasn't on purpose
That you caused me pain
      And I forgive you

I hope you are able to heal one day too
      Don't even try to deny it
I know because
Hurt people, hurt people
I've done my share of hurting
      And endured just as much

Glimpses

In the past, you've said
    "I'm a bad friend"
    "I don't deserve you"
And that's not true
No one else has done for me
    The things you did for me
You were everything I asked for in a best friend

My mind felt heavy the other night
Filled with good memories
That I didn't want to forget

I started writing them down
Before I knew it, it had been two hours
And I had written down fifty-two happy memories
    Things I missed about you
    Things I missed about us
    Things I missed about our friendship

As time went on
I think we both lost ourselves
I'd occasionally still see glimpses of you
And I'm holding on to those moments for dear life
Because when we lost ourselves
    My best friend went away too

Changed

Things are different now
I know that
I think both of us needed it
        Change

Hindsight is 20/20
And judging by the states we were in
We probably should have fallen further apart

The memories I've made since are good
But they have a tinge of blue.
        Because they are missing you
I find and chase my moments of joy
But I've already spent so much of my life unhappy
        And I want to keep enjoying my life
I just wish you could be a part of it too

Past Tense

I explained my situation.
I thought you understood.
I believed you when you said you were different.
I trusted you.
You convinced me that you were safe.

Every time I talk about us now,
It's all in past tense,
As if my mind is telling me
We have no right now.
We have no future.

Instead of *being*
You *were*.
Now I am questioning everything.

Supposed

You were never supposed to be the one who left
You were never supposed to abandon me
You were never supposed to make me cry
You were never supposed to hurt me
You were never supposed to fade away

You were supposed to always be there for me

We were supposed to be best friends
We were supposed to be there for each other
It was supposed to be forever
You weren't supposed to leave
I don't know what I'm supposed to do now
But I suppose all of those
Have turned into "no's"
And I suppose I'll do those things alone

Too Good

I always knew forever was too good to be true.
And I should have known better
When you said it'd last for two,
That it wasn't a storm I could weather.

And Counting

June 27, 2016
The first day we said we'd be best friends
Since then it's been
Five years, eleven months, and thirty days
> That's 2,190 days
> That's 52,560 hours
> That's 3,153,600 minutes
> That's 189,216,000 seconds
That's not the number I want to talk about

November 14, 2020
That's the last time I saw you in person
That was the last time we had a conversation
That was 589 days ago
> And counting
But that's not the number I want to talk about

In those 589 days
There was a worldwide pandemic
There was family drama
My books got delivered
My grandma passed away
I didn't allow myself to feel anything
> It was all too much
I stopped writing altogether

I unexpectedly lost my aunt
I cried a lot
      Alone
      A lot
Over the course of these days I wrote five letters
      I got one back
Those aren't the numbers I want to talk about either

The only number I care about is
Zero
Zero was the number of times we saw each other
Zero was the number of conversations
Zero was the number of check-ins
Zero of those things in the 589 days
      Were you a part of
Zero of those days went by without me
      Hurting
      Crying
      Missing you
      Needing you
      Needing someone
Zero of those days went by without me thinking
      Did I do something wrong?
      Do you miss me?
      Do you even love me anymore?
      Did you ever?
      I wish you were with me
Zero is the number of days I asked for space

But I gave you 589
            And counting
Zero is the number that matters

In total, it's been 2,190 days of friendship
589 of those have consisted of zeroes
So in case you're confused
Let me be very clear

If you don't want to be friends, so be it
            It's not like we've been acting like it
But if you do
It will take a lot of work
And we will be starting at
Zero

Lost Things Found Better

You invited me over tonight
It was out of the blue
It made me anxious
        In fact, I sat in front of the house
        My normal parking spot
        And I almost decided to go back home
But my desire to see you eclipsed every other anxiety
I had
And it will every time

I was greeted with a hug in the driveway
        As usual
Before tonight I thought that I didn't want that
        Us to act normal
But that was before I remembered
How much I missed you

My entrance to the house prompted a
"No fucking way"
"Holy shit, look who it is"
And even more hugs
        My second family
It had been a while since I felt that welcome any-
where

It was like we hadn't skipped a beat
I know that's how true friendships are
        I was so scared we'd lost that
The ice didn't need to be broken
It felt natural to talk, joke, and laugh
        All things that I hadn't done in a long time

Adjusting

All it took was one night
For me to feel it all again
I had been in a drought
          You were thirst quenching
Everything in me wanted more
But I am trying to be better
I am learning
          And I have learned
I'm growing
          And I have grown

We jumped in so fast
But what comes quick, goes quick
          That was our flaw from the beginning
Our whole lives were ahead of us
Two eighteen-year-olds with no fucking clue of
what's to come
We crashed and burned
          Hard and fast

Maybe next time
          If there is a next time
We ease our way in
At a comfortable pace
          Then, we'll be able to fly

Offered Honestly

I just need to say it
It hurt my feelings
Being left behind
      In the dark
      Alone
But I shouldn't be surprised
No one pays attention to what I say.

I always accommodate your schedule
Why can't you reciprocate?
It makes me feel lesser than everyone else.

It's a small thing
But those can accumulate
Time and time again I've tolerated
      The back-handed comments
      The interruptions
      The gaslighting
      The lack of consideration
      The obvious signs of no one giving a fuck
This was the cherry on top
      The last straw.

I'm telling you this in an effort to save our friendship
And I am hoping that by sharing how it made me feel
It won't happen again.

When I Did

"If you need me, please don't hesitate to reach out"
Bullshit.

I did the hard part
I told you
I reached out
And you left me hanging
So here I am
          Foolishly
Still waiting.

Absence

I wouldn't have made a different of version of you
If the real you were there for me like you promised.
We only consider alternatives when the originals fail.

It's just hard because you didn't betray me.
You didn't pull the rug from underneath me.
You didn't say anything that hurt me.
We didn't argue or have a fight.

You just weren't there.

I needed you
And you weren't there.
It hurt like hell.

Needs vs. Wants

What if I don't need you?
What if I just **want** to be around my best friend?
      What if I just **want** to have a conversation?
      What if I don't **want** to be alone?
Let's get one thing straight
I don't need you
      I don't **need** anyone
I just want my friend back.

Feel free to let me know if you find **her**.

Pump the Brakes

I trusted you
Without precaution,
No hesitation.
Experience told me not to—
I wish I had listened.

Please, Show Me

All I wanted was some kind of emotion
      Remorse
      Anger
      Regret
Something to show me that I mattered
To show me you knew you could have done better
      Could have been there for me

It hurts more to see you go on like nothing hap-
pened
Than it does to not see you anymore
Did you even care at all?
      In the slightest?

Which Is It?

I used to be so sure.
Certain that you knew me
        That you saw me
When no one else did

Yet, I've told myself repeatedly that you don't
        That you can't give me what I wanted
        That you couldn't give me what I needed
        That you weren't there
So which is it?

Independent

I thought I'd have someone to lean on
     When the other shoe finally dropped,
But I was all alone when shit hit the fan.
     Forced to get myself through it.

I don't know how to need you anymore—
Everything I thought I needed you for
I didn't.

And I don't.

Past to the Present

When you look at the past
Then look at the present
You know it didn't last
And wonder how we broke it

We were once best friends
And we never thought it'd end
But nothing went as planned
And we were no longer hand in hand
We'd just fight and fight
With no end in sight

We'd make up the next day
And the problems would all go away
I'd stick up for you any day
Protect you in every way

That one fight was the end
We were no longer friends
I wish we could talk
But I can't bear it
Away I have to walk
I just can't stand it

You're begging me not to go
    All I want to do is stay
But I have to say no
    I hate that things went this way

Friendship

I am looking for something to say
I never thought about when it would end
Now we are going our separate ways
But you will always be my friend

No matter what, I'll always care
And no matter what, in my heart
You will always be there
Even as we drift apart

These words aren't strong enough to show
My true feelings, but they're all I have to give
And I hope you always know
I'll be there for you as long as we live

Free Fall

I can't just let stuff go
It's not who I am
If I do
I'll just end up hating both of us

This weighs on me like a breakup
       And in the worst ways it is
I trusted you
I gave you my baggage
I opened up to you
       Yet here we are
Maybe you weren't listening
Maybe you didn't care
Maybe you were unaware
       In the end the reason doesn't matter

There are moments
       Scarce and brief
That I forget about where we are
       What we've become
But I get snapped back to reality in an instance
And it all comes flooding back in

Things changed because
I was the only one

Fighting for us
     A friendship that may have never been there
     In the first place

So though I may not let go
     Even though I should
I will loosen my grip

Bittersweet

I had a really hard week
I struggled a lot
It felt like everyone was against me
      I felt inadequate
I was juggling a different conflict
Every time I turned a corner

I entertained the idea of asking you
If I could stop by
      Not necessarily to hang out
      I didn't really want to talk
At the time I just didn't want to be alone
I wanted to feel safe
I just wanted to be with my best friend
      To see your face
      Hear your voice
      Get a hug
I knew you'd be able to give me
The comfort that I wanted and needed
And if you made me feel as if everything else melted
away
      Even just for a second
It would have been worth it

It's bittersweet to know
You're still that person for me
The one I look to
>   For the slightest bit of light
>   To lead me out from the darkness

I ended up staying silent
>   Maybe out of pride, still, for some reason
>   Maybe because I didn't want your pity
>   Maybe because I'm still trying to respect
your boundaries
But that night, missing you almost hurt too much
For me to care about any of those things

I almost called you that night
Maybe next time I will

White Flag

I've been trying to straddle two diverging paths
  Moving on
  Holding on
Obviously, that's not sustainable
But the deepest cut
Is that I was wrong about you
I thought I had you figured out
  Thought I had won the lottery
But I went bankrupt instead

You aren't the one I was looking for
I wish you were
I give in
I'm done fighting

Slipping

My knuckles are white from the tension
I can feel my pulse in my fingertips
I'm losing my grip
      But you're already gone.

When I would read your notes
I used to be able to hear your voice
As if you were saying the words to me again
      But now I can't get the pitch just right
The boom of your laugh is merely an echo these
days.
Songs have to be skipped over
      Because they remind me too much of you
Once happy memories have hues of blue.

I am refusing to believe the truth I already know.
I am trying to keep you from slipping away
While you're telling me to let go
      In every way except for out loud.

Seasons of You

The weather is beginning to cool
And the leaves starting to change
Backyard barbeques and bonfires
Allow us to try to hold onto the last bit of summer
       I can't help but think of you

Snow falls silently and delicately
The trees are bare and exposed
They're patiently waiting for their turn to bloom
The days are short and nights are long
Christmas lights line the sidewalks
       That I walk down alone

The grass grows greener
The trees are full of fresh green foliage
Everyone is itching with spring fever
Sunlight is refracting off of the rain droplets on
flower petals
I'm singing in the rain
       But dancing without you

The freedom that comes with long summer days
Storms go as quickly as they appear
With warm summer evenings
And late nights that lead to slow mornings
      Sitting with the nostalgia of summers past

One day you were here and the next you weren't
For a while, I could still hear you
I could still feel your presence
And as time goes on, that feeling fades away
      But the memory of you never will

Memories can't love me back
They can't wipe my tears
But right now, memories are all I have
And I am clinging on to those memories
So like you,
      They don't leave me too

I Do

I occasionally drive past your street
To see if any new sense memories pop up
I miss all the things I used to hate
They drove me nuts
But I'd do anything
To get mad about them again
       I shouldn't miss you, but I do

I wonder if you have the same thoughts I do
The ones that just invade your mind
In the middle of doing something
I can always feel the vacancy
Of when I celebrated my birthday without you
Or when I looked at Christmas lights alone
You weren't there when I needed a shoulder to cry
on
       I shouldn't miss you, but I do

I didn't just lose you
When we were friends
I spent more time with your family
Than my own
Our friends felt like they had to pick sides
And I don't see them anymore either
       I shouldn't miss you, but I do

Every time I let someone in
I get a reminder of why I shouldn't have
In the beginning, my mind says *be careful*
But my heart lets out a thirst quenching *finally*
Now my brain is trying to console
My broken heart
        With *I told you so*'s

I shouldn't miss you
So maybe I'll stop

Letting Go

They say you grip tighter before letting go
      Because you can feel it slipping away
I held on to you
      At least I tried
I pulled out all the stops
I tried everything I could think of
      To keep you
      To make you feel loved
      To show you I cared

I asked the universe repeatedly
To give me what I needed
      To be there for me
      To be reliable
      To make me laugh again
      To make me feel safe again
      To feel like I belong
      To be heard
      To be seen
      To be loved
Only to realize I already have it
I have everything
All that I have asked for
I just couldn't see it

Because I was so focused on holding on
To you
But now it's time to let go
        Really let go

I want to say thank you
        For everything you gave me
        For everything you did for me
        For always reminding me I am enough
I want to say I'm sorry
        For the things I couldn't give you
        For all the things I didn't say enough
        For all the things I did say
        For not being strong enough to hold on

I love you
(Inhale)
(Exhale)

Save Your Breath

Save your breath
>I've been here before
Save your breath
>I've heard this before
Save your breath
>I've been left out before
Save your breath
>I've been abandoned before
Save your breath
>I've lost someone before
Save your breath
>I've been disappointed before
Save your breath
>I've been led on before
Save your breath
>I've been laughed at before
Save your breath
>I've been on the outside my whole life

Save your breath
This situation is nothing new to me
It's always been the same old story
There is nothing you can say
	That will help me feel better
	That will make a difference

So save your breath
	And your time
Don't waste it on me
I know how to put myself back together

Attention

Help me understand
Maybe it's because the rest of our friends are men
        And that's the kind of attention you like
Maybe it's me
Because I'm smothering or over-protective
Whatever label you want to give it today.

When I see you having fun with other people
I think, "Man, I don't make them that happy"
And how is that supposed to make me feel?
When I'm the one constantly there for you
        Trying to help.
But they get all the attention
        All of the affection.

Maybe I care too much
Maybe the only way to get your attention
        Is to not give you mine
And you know I'm not capable of that
But if I could pull it off
I'd choose it in a heartbeat.

Poison Apple

I guess she only spent time with me
To get face time with him
      I've been on this rollercoaster before

I applaud her technique
She did what she set out to do
      Tricked me into trusting
      Got what she wanted from me
      Got the guy
She used me
She complains about communication
But ghosted me when she got what she wanted
There were times where a true friend
Would have asked how I was doing
      But all I got was silence

A rotten apple spoils the bunch
And I've come too far
To be spoiled from one person's actions.

I hope it was worth it.

Horns or Halos?

Am I the bad guy here?
Does it make me the bad guy
For wanting the best for him
      Even if it is not her?
      Even if he's happy with her?
      Even if he doesn't see it?

Am I the bad guy
If I tell him he could do better
      Even if he loves her?

Am I the bad guy
If I tell him his relationship is toxic
      When I think he can't see it?

Or do I become the bad guy
If I see it
And don't say a word?

Am I the bad guy
If I can tell he acts different,
      Jovial
When she isn't around?

Am I the bad guy
If I take a step back
Knowing he did nothing wrong
        Except fall in love?

If I say how I feel
        What I think
        What I have observed
He'll feel like he has to pick sides
And I don't want him to have to
        But she'd be quick to make him
        And be sure that he picks hers
From the outside, the stakes are high
In fact, I have everything to lose
        And nothing to gain
I could tell him my thoughts
Plant the seed
Maybe he'd see it eventually
Then thank me for looking out

The other option is I tell him
And he never sees it
        I lose my best friend
        But hell, I'm already starting to aren't I?

So am I the bad guy if I speak up?
Or would it be worse to hold my tongue?

I guess instead of asking if I'm the bad guy
I should be asking myself who I want to be in the
narrative:
The supportive friend with a shoulder to lean on
Or the devil on your shoulder
Pointing out all the flaws you can't see

Biting My Tongue

It never felt like it would go the distance
She wanted someone that he wasn't
She's tried to change him
And he shouldn't have to change a damn thing
If she really loved him, she'd feel the same way

Now he's acting out of character
And I want to tell him I think it's a cry for help
    But it's not my business

Expecting change is unrealistic
Compromising is doable
    You can't be all take, no give

I'd be willing to jeopardize my relationship with her
    Or what's left of it
But my relationship with shared friends
And my relationship with him would be at stake as
well
    That is something I can't risk

Broken

I know I could call you up
      Walk through your front door
And we'd fall right back in

The sad and scary part is
I'm not sure that's what I want
You made me feel things
I never thought you'd make me feel

Broken.

I Hope It's Really Over

It was this thing that seemed intangible
So far off in the distance, it didn't seem real
Something we'd joke about but never reach
I never feared it because I never saw it coming
It was never supposed to happen
   How are you supposed to prepare for the end?

Maybe I'll be able to listen to your favorite bands again
   The ones that made our summer soundtracks
Without holding back tears
Without feeling the weight of the hole in my heart
Without replaying our "greatest hits" in my brain
Without the shadow of you

Maybe one day I won't feel the sting of the silence
   Once you found someone else to lean on
Maybe I'll learn it had nothing to do with me
And everything to do with you
Maybe I'll stop beating myself up
For what I thought I did to you
Maybe I'll start letting people in again
   Trusting people again
   Loving people again

I hope I can go to a restaurant on your side of town
  Without checking to see if it is you walking in
the door
I hope the color returns to my life
  Running off all the black, white, and gray
I hope someone new pops in my head
  When I'm drunk and want someone to talk to
I hope you eventually fade to a blur
When I recall our happy memories together
  So I don't feel the pain of you
I hope the echoes of your voice and your laugh
  Run out of room to bounce around in my mind

I hope I have enough love for myself to let you go
And stop torturing myself
I hope one day I can burn all the letters
  Take down all the photos
And allow myself to heal completely
  Anything to stop me from reopening the wounds
I hope I smile again as big as I once did
  When it was you making me smile
I hope you move far away
  So I can drive past your street without a second
thought
I hope I'm able to pick up this pencil
  Without being scared of what it may write
  Without streaking the paper with tears

I hope I can go back to hating Halloween
I hope I can dance again
I hope I'm able to convince myself
        It was just a bunch of "Little White Lies"
I hope June 27th becomes a regular day again
I hope I stop wasting my life waiting for you to
come back
I hope you remember that I love you
        But you remember that you love me enough
to leave me alone

I used to hope that every text I got was from you
        Now I hope it is anyone but you
I used to pray I'd never have to know life without
you
        Now I'm praying to know peace after you
And I hope this time it is really over
Because if it's not
I'd be the first to sign up to be hurt again
So please, for my sake
Let it be over

Different

I wish I could make you understand
How much I miss you
There's a hole in my chest nothing else can fill
I can feel despair passing through with every breeze

If I could go back in time with what I know now
If it meant we could still be in each other's lives
If it meant we'd still be friends
        I'd do it all differently

But would I really feel different,
If it was this version of you in front of me?
Or would the mere presence of you
Make all the difference in the world?

The Price

At the end of the day
You won't be able to say I wasn't there for you.
I will not let you walk all over me
        Push me to the side.

If you need me, I'll be there,
But not at the cost of myself.
Don't mistake my love for weakness.
I know what I deserve
And I'm done forgetting it.

Phantom Conversations

"We suffer more in imagination than in reality"
—SENECA

Phantom Conversations Over Coffee

About two months into the silence
You asked me to get coffee the next weekend
I hesitated
        But I agreed

All week I was anxious about it
So much so, my brain couldn't rest
Every dead moment was filled with "what ifs"
So I decided to just let the scenarios run wild
        Maybe that way, they'd go away

I wrote it all out
The conversations I convinced myself were inevitable
        All the while, bawling my eyes out
All of them followed the same framework
Starting with small talk
Ending with me walking away
Alone

We never ended up getting coffee
So our future will remain a mystery
        For now at least
But just know I agonize over that day
        On repeat
That we meet up to say what we need to say
And I have to be the one
To walk away

Phantom Conversations: What You Know

Hey
What do you want?
>*Do I have to want something to see you?*
That's usually the case.
>*That's not fair.*
Are you going to tell me why you're here?
>*I don't know if I want to anymore.*
Great, thanks for wasting my time.
>*Wait!*
>*Listen, I know we haven't talked in a while,*
>*But that can't be all my fault.*
>*Communication is a two-way street.*
Except when it isn't, right?
>*Meaning?*
You told me you needed space,
Whatever the fuck that means.
Then you say communication is a two-way street.
Bullshit.
That's not communication.
That's closing the door until **you** open it.
>*I told you if you needed me, you could…*
Everyone knows that is cliché, courtesy bullshit.
I've been at home thinking I did something wrong.
Crying.

Hating myself.
Struggling for months.
>   *Do you expect me to just know all of this?*
>   *Do you think I can read minds?*
Good point. Let's go through what you do know.
I told you about all the times people lied to me.
All the times people abandoned me.
And how those experiences affected me.
Yet, here we are living the same damn thing.
When I was telling you all of that,
Were you listening?
Did you care?
One of those answers is clearly "no"
Pick your poison.
Either way, I'm out a friend.
>   *I swear I didn't…*
I have trust issues.
And you damn well knew that.
I'm not angry.
I could never be mad at you.
I am hurt.
And there is a difference.
I just want you to understand that you caused me
pain.

And I feel it every damn day,
And if things ever do "go back to normal"
It will be a long time from now,
And I hate that.
Excuse me.
(Leaves.)

Phantom Conversations: After All

So how have you been?
Is this really what we're going to do?
What do you mean?
Are we just going to act like the last five months
didn't happen?
I asked how you've been.
Fine. I've been better.
I didn't come here to talk about me.
You asked me to come here.
So, what do **you** want to say?
I just wanted to see you.
We haven't hung out in a while.
And who's fault is that?
I didn't know it was anyone's fault
But I suppose you're going to say mine.
Do you disagree?
I mean yes and no…
Yes, and no?!
I'm busy, I work a lot.
This.
This is why I was hesitant about this all week.
Why is that?
Because you fuck around with everyone's minds,
Then act like nothing happened.

It's like if you wait long enough
All the pain you caused will go away—
It doesn't.
>*Pain? What the hell are you talking about?*
Pain. Yes pain.
Make fun of me all you want
For being sensitive and all that bullshit
But you hurt me.
>*I am so...*
I know.
You're sorry.
You had no idea.
You've had your own shit going on.
Fair.
But that doesn't make other people's shit disappear.
>*And yours doesn't make mine disappear.*
I know that.
But **you** disappeared!
And that is the part that is not okay!
You said you'd be there.
So what the fuck?
>*I told you if you needed...*
Here we go again.
>*What?*
"If you need me," what kind of bullshit is that?
By the way
I did tell you that I needed you
In September, and do you remember what you said?

Don't worry if you don't, I'll tell you.

"Soon."

Last week was the first time since then that you even talked to me.

You were the one that wanted space.

I gave it to you.

I didn't text you because I didn't need you.

I just **wanted** my best friend.

I just **wanted** someone to talk to.

I **wanted** to be around someone other than myself.

  I…

I'm going home now.

  I came here because I don't want space anymore.

Maybe space was a good idea after all.

Phantom Conversations: Done

So how are you?
How have you been?
Are we sharing feelings now?
What do you mean?
Well, usually when I share feelings,
I get called sensitive and shit
So I'm just confirming whether we're making small talk
Or if you're being genuine and want me to be honest.
I always want you to be honest.
Well, in September I said I was having a rough time.
Said I needed a "best friend day"
And you said "soon."
I'm still waiting on soon.
Hey…
I'm not done.
You told me to stop asking if you were okay
Or asking if you needed help
Because you "aren't the kind of person to accept it."
I don't think this was a good idea.
Oh, I'm still not done.
In November, I finally got the courage to tell you
I was feeling neglected
And feeling like a safety net friend.
You said "I'm not doing that"

Immediately invalidating my feelings
And proving my point.
Then you told me "Just because I need space, doesn't
mean I love you less"
But kept trying to talk to me.
I don't know what to do with that.
>*Okay, I get it.*
>*I don't know what you want me to say.*

Please, don't say anything.
It's what you're best at.
Don't worry, I'm almost done.
Remember when you lied?
Broke any trust we ever had?
Don't you hate when people tell you to trust them,
but you can't?
Me too.
>*Of course, it's about…*

Yes! God!
I spend all this time explaining all the times I've
needed my best friend
So, it **has** to be about someone else!
I don't even know why I'm here
Trying to salvage a friendship
With someone I don't even recognize

Who the hell are you?
> *Where are you going?*

Away.

Didn't you want space?

Wish granted.
> *But I don't want space anymore.*
> *That's why I'm here.*

Why?

Because no one else is giving you attention?

Please just leave me alone.

I'm done.

Phantom Conversations: Make Believe

Hey
> *Hey, how are you?*

I'm okay, how about yourself?
> *Good, I'm fine.*

That's good. What about the family? The dogs?
> *All good. Driving me nuts as always, but good.*

That's nice to hear
> *You seem better*
> *Not that something was wrong before*
> *But more yourself*
> *Calmer.*

Well, I've had a lot of time to myself to think
Straighten things out in my mind.
> *Amazing*
> *So, can we please go back to being friends now?*

About that…
> *I've missed you.*

Look, as I was sifting through my thoughts
I realized I came up with a version of you
That doesn't exist
Then I got upset when you didn't live up to it
Which isn't fair.
> *You don't have to apologize.*
> *It's okay…*

I'm not apologizing.
    Oh.
The person in my mind,
That was my best friend.
She was there for me when I needed her
And even when I didn't know I needed her
She chose me
Repeatedly
Unconditionally
But she is gone.
She is not you.
    But I'm right here.
I used to see glimpses of her in you
But as time went on
I saw less and less of her
Until we reached where we are now.
I tried to save it
Tried everything I could think of
But all that did was make you
Push me away more.
    I don't like the sound of this.
You were my best friend
But to you, I was just another person.
I was fighting for a friendship
That wasn't real.
I never thought I'd be the butt of the one-sided
friendship jokes.
    It's not one-sided.

Isn't it?
Let's face it. We were never best friends.
You were mine,
But I was never yours.
  If you felt this way, why'd you agree to meet?
Because I'm not like you.
I can tell you how I'm feeling to your face.
Plus, you said you needed to talk
And despite how you've treated me,
I care about you.
I just thought you cared about me too.
  I do love you, you know.
You say that
But it takes more than you saying it
For me to believe it.

Just Walk Away

Walking away was the easiest part
I was so caught up in the fight
I didn't even notice that you didn't care
It's not about winning or losing
          There is no winning in this kind of fight
It's about healing
And that's what you get
By choosing to walk away

Phantom Conversations: Debate

The argument could always be made
"You never asked"
>*Neither did you.*
"You didn't tell me"
>*I didn't know I had to.*
"I still love you"
>*I don't believe you.*

Phantom Conversations: Change of Scenery

I need to redecorate my room.
> *That was a little random.*

I used to find it so comforting.
> *Do you not anymore?*

I'm sure it is comforting to whoever it was meant for.
> *You're losing me.*
> *These are your letters and pictures.*

Do you know why I love my birthday so much?
> *You are all over the place right now*
> *Are you okay?*

Humor me.
> *Alright, why do you love your birthday?*

It's my day.
> *Of course.*

The one day I'm the main character.
The one day I'm noticed.
> *You're noticed.*

No one gives a shit about me.
I'm invisible.
I don't even recognize myself.
I see friends, family, the places I've gone,
But there's a stranger there too.
The smiles, the laughter, the closeness.

I don't recognize it, I don't feel it, I don't remember it.
    Come here.
Please don't hug me right now.
    I'm trying to help.
It is not helping.
    What do you want me to do?
There isn't anything you can do.
    I'm not going to listen to all this and do nothing.
Why not?
It's what you've been doing all along.
    Excuse me?!
Never mind.
I have to start redecorating.

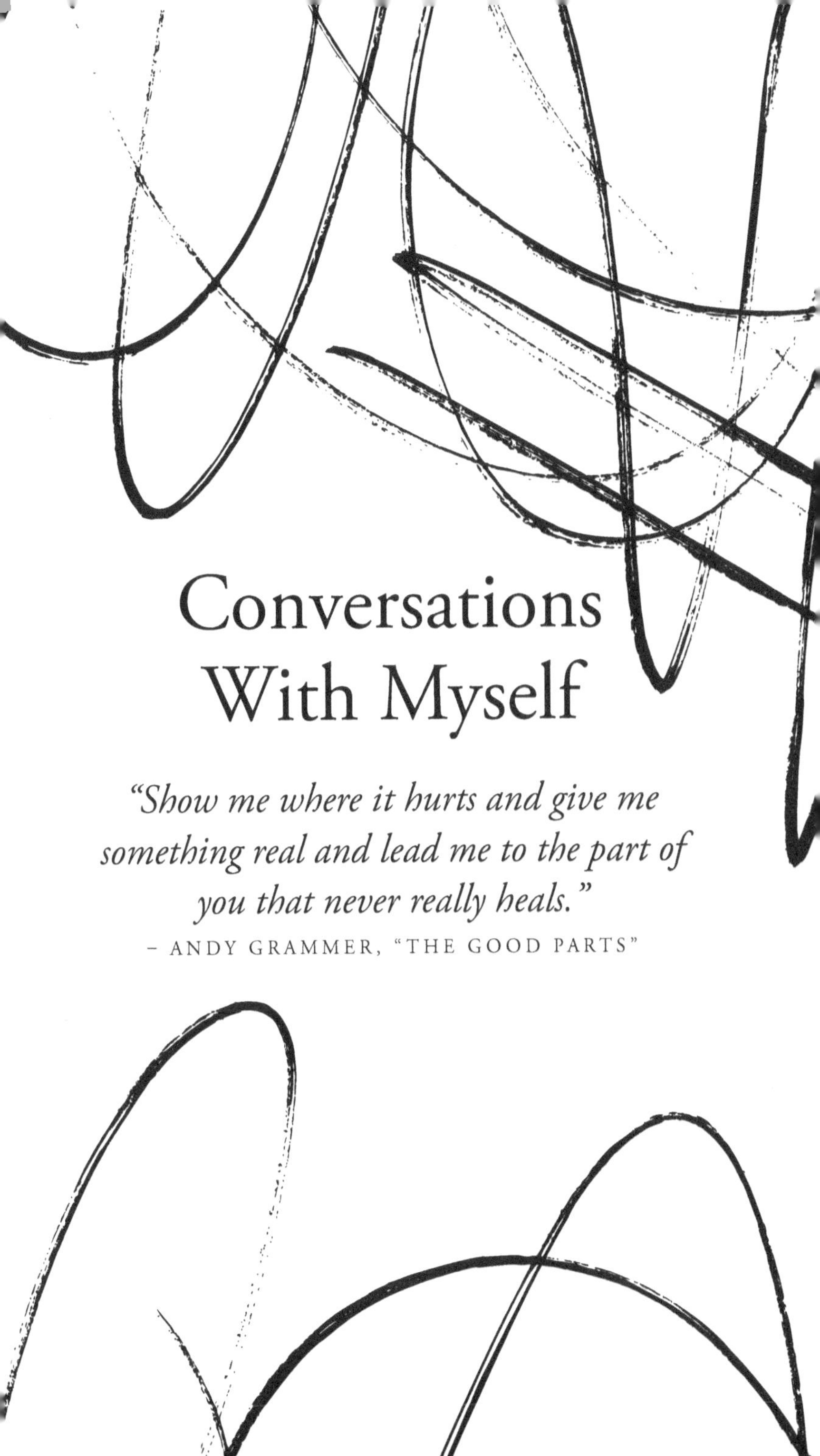

Conversations With Myself

"Show me where it hurts and give me something real and lead me to the part of you that never really heals."

– ANDY GRAMMER, "THE GOOD PARTS"

Conversations with Myself: The Beginning

It's been so long
Now I finally get to see you
I had it all planned out
      A place
      A time
      The conversation
Then I didn't hear from you

Maybe you're still closing
Surely if something came up
You would have told me
You've had no trouble with that in the past
I'll just run my errands

I picked up what I needed
Started the car
Put it in drive
      I bet there's a pop-up event
      You're too busy to tell me to wait
      Or you still have customers
      People don't pay attention to store hours
      One time I waited until six-thirty
      I'll drive by to see if you are still there

The lights were off.
        Car was gone.

To your house, I went
When I pulled up to my spot
Your car was there
Empty
You were already inside
        Could you have forgotten?
        No way
        We made these plans yesterday
I asked you to come outside
        You changed your clothes already
        You looked relaxed
You forgot

Conversations with Myself: Waiting for You

It's getting late
I should probably head home soon
The moon is rising
The stars are shining
The restaurant closes in an hour from now
Will we even have time to eat?
Maybe I'll just wait five more minutes

> *You promised it wouldn't happen anymore*
> *But here I am, once again*
> *Waiting for you*
> *Checking my watch, ten minutes late*
> *Checking my phone, no calls, no texts*
> *I don't know why I keep checking, there's no use*
> *Sleep—maybe that's the answer*

That quiets my thoughts for a little
Even though I know you're awake

> *You probably got a better offer*
> *One that smiles a little easier*
> *One who cries a little less*
> *One who has fewer scars*
> *One who isn't a mess*

Maybe you just don't want me in your life
Maybe I expected more than you could give
I drove you away
I was too overwhelming
Should I ask or just assume?
If I assume it could break my heart
But the answer to my question could hurt even more
I look at my watch again
Still no sign of you
Maybe there's traffic
I'll wait a little longer

I'm sorry that I'm needy
I just want to feel loved
I'm sorry that I ask a lot of questions
I want to know how you are
I'm sorry that I seem angry
I feel so distant when I want to be close
You see, we think we have all the time in the world
That's a lie
Do I really want to spend time waiting on you?
Is it worth it?
Are you worth it?
Tomorrow isn't promised

> *And I say all this*
> *So that if tomorrow doesn't come for one of us*
> *At least you'll know*
> > *I worried about you. Every day.*
> > *I waited for you. Every time.*
> > *I thought about you. Every day.*
> > *I needed you. All the time.*
> *If we do get to see tomorrow*
> *We'll ride the rollercoaster all over again*

"Hey. I'm so tired, I don't think I can make it. I'm sorry. Next time, I promise."
"Something came up, I can't come."
"I just want to do my own thing tonight."

> *I got the best news today*
> *You were the only person I wanted to tell*
> *What's the point of gaining the world*
> *When you have no one to share it with?*
> *I really needed to talk*
> *Today was a hard day*
> *I didn't want to be alone*
> *I don't trust myself*

It's okay
All good
Maybe some other time

I say
Time to go home
Alone
Brokenhearted

Crushed spirit
Just because I can carry it, doesn't mean it isn't heavy
I'll spend another night
Wondering what I did wrong
Wondering why I wasn't enough

I know it sounds ridiculous, but I can't help it
That's where my mind goes
Every time
I get my hopes up
And you just make them crumble

Please hear this
Don't say "I'm sorry"
Don't say "I miss you"
Don't say "I promise"
Don't say "Yes"
Don't say "I love you"
Unless you mean it

My heart is naïve enough to believe you
And I can't bear any more hurt

Conversations with Myself: Trusting or Nothing

People tell me they love me everyday
How do I know they mean it?
After all, words are just air and sound waves
      Or markings on an object
      Or pixels on a screen
We arrange words to define other man-made words
And call it language
If words were the foundation of language
      Yet they are all subjective in meaning
How could we understand anything?

How can I trust what others say to me?
Maybe I can look at their actions
      See if they match what they are telling me
Even if they do match, does that mean it's true?
We control our words and actions
So what does it mean if they match?
      If the actions match fake words,
      Then are the actions fake as well?
If they don't match
Which do I trust?
      Are they telling the truth?
      Are they showing the truth?
People will tell me to trust my gut

But what if that's a lie too?

Most of my conversations
Are with the voice inside my head
      It's a daily thing
And I have no say in the matter
Most of the time, the voice is blunt
Says things I don't want to hear
Sometimes it's comforting
        Which is very rare
One thing is certain
The voice is never quiet
          Does it tell me the truth or lies?
If it aligns with what others say
Does that make it more true?
If none of them match up
How am I supposed to I know what to believe?

All of these questions
Creating a constant internal conflict
I can't trust other people
I can't even trust myself
What is one to do
When they quite literally
Trust no one

I love words
Words have such power when spoken

Such beauty when written
Such weight when heard
Such clarity when sang
They can bring you to the depths of depression
Or the elevation of euphoria
It just depends on the day

Trusting others is always a debate
Trusting myself is impossible
I choose to trust nothing
It may be exhausting
      But nothing will never lie to me
      Nothing will never hurt me
      Nothing will never leave
So nothing is what I'll be

Conversations with Myself: My Own Enemy

It all started with a dream
I stretched out my arms
Seeking love, comfort, warmth
      Something
But I never felt a single thing
They reached out with their words
Yet, those too, failed

The words
I know you meant them, but
They weren't enough for me, they were just air
      My ears heard them
      My brain understood them
      But I didn't feel them
      My heart still longed for love
When I woke, my only company
Was the voice inside my head

It's all fun and games until it becomes real
      Happiness is inconsistent and that's okay
I'm drowning under the wave of words we aren't
saying
      Be stronger than the storm
I don't know what to do

Asking for help doesn't make you weak
What are you right now?
    I'm a work in progress, but I'm trying
Why can't you love me back?
    My heart will hold you even when my arms cannot
I want my own space too, but I need you
    Be strong enough to heal yourself, even when it hurts
    Stand tall. Head up.
I'm here alone in the dark
    Be like the moon; inspire when you're far from full
    Be like the stars; shine through the darkness
I hate that I'm still hoping
    Everything is going to be alright
I thought you forgot about me
    I'll never leave you behind
No reason to stay is a good reason to go
    Stay
I tried to be what you wanted me to be
    Be enough for yourself first, the rest can wait
What if I fall?
    What if you fly?

When I needed you, where were you?
When I'm struggling like this, why do you let me?
I'd drop everything for you
And you said you would do the same
          Were you just saying that because you
thought that's what I wanted to hear?
What happened to "don't bottle it up"?
What happened to "talk to me"?
Can I trust you?

I'm okay
          Not everything you think is the truth
For once, I want to be the one who is **fought for**
          *I'll show you maximum effort when you prove
you are worth it*
After all the asking, no answer becomes the answer
you've been looking for
At some point you have to let go of what you
thought should happen
And live in what is happening
          *We create our own heartbreaks through expec-
tations*
I'm done saving myself
          Feel what you need to feel, then let go

You said: "This isn't fair"
"There are so many things I could say and want to
say to try to make this better for you
But the biggest thing is for you to feel those words
and believe them"
"The version of me that you created in your head is
not my responsibility"
"I'm not the enemy here"

As my story ended
I realized I created this issue
I am the problem
And I was the villain
All along

Conversations with Myself: In the Dust

I get left out a lot
I've been whispered about
I've been laughed at
I've been lied to
It is a terrible feeling
I thought there could be nothing worse
I was wrong

I started getting left out by friends
People I introduced to other friends
      Started spending time together without me
I stopped getting invited
It made me feel unwanted
Cue the downward spiral
     What did you do this time?
     They don't like you.
     You don't have friends.

I feel stuck
Stagnant
I'm finding ways to pass the time
     Ways to keep myself busy
Trying not to think about what people are doing
without me

Trying to be happy for them
        For living their dreams
        For having fun
While I'm sitting at home
Alone

Please don't leave me behind.

Conversations with Myself: Buyer's Remorse

There's a voice inside my head
Always telling me I'm not good enough
          Telling me I don't belong
That feeling seeps into every aspect of my life
It's breaking me down
Tearing me up from the inside out

You're pretending to have fun, they can tell.
They don't love you.
How could they?

Maybe if I could just start over
I could make it better
          I could make better choices
          I could be happy
          I could love myself

Unfortunately, we don't get do-overs in life
          And that fucking sucks

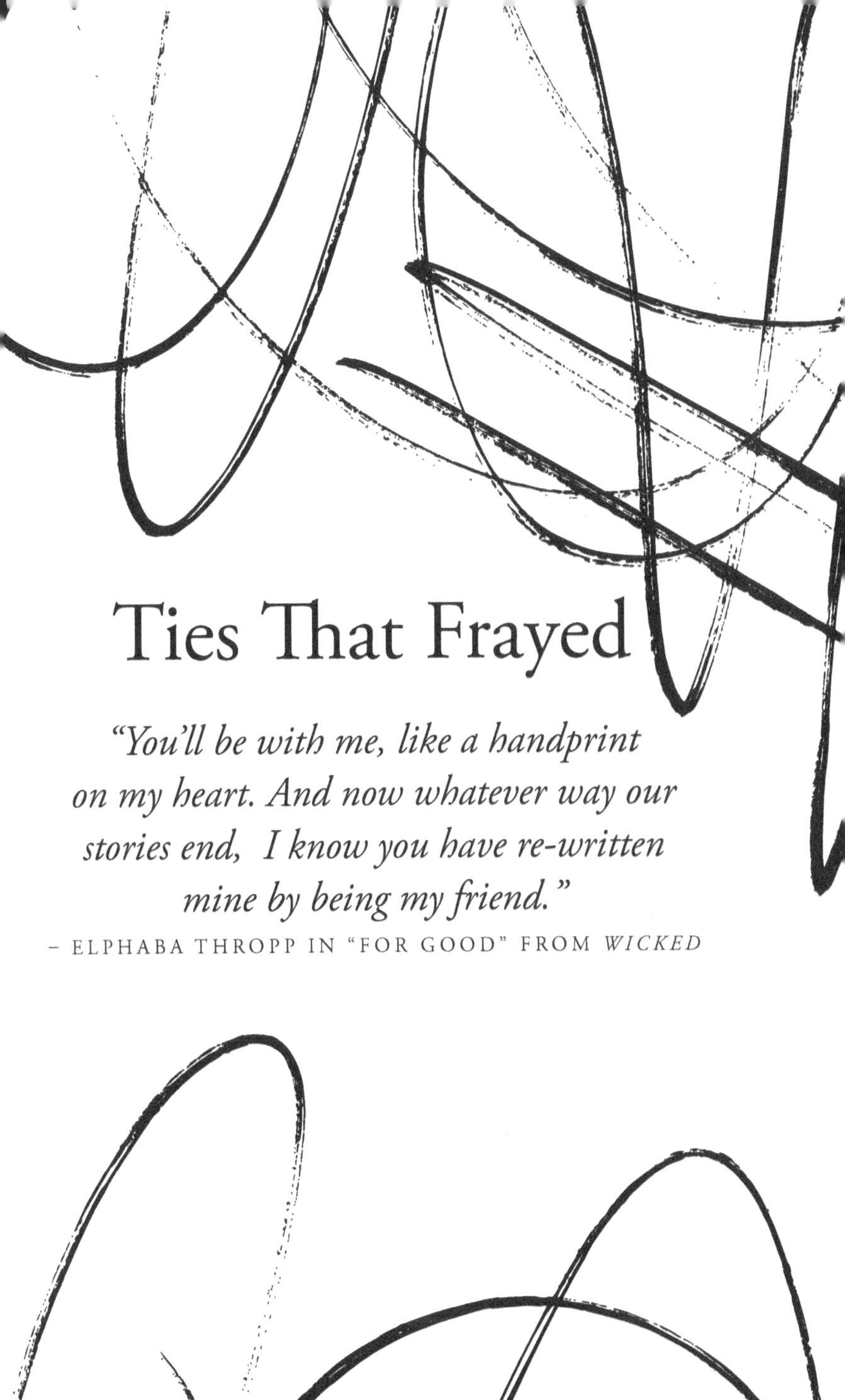

Ties That Frayed

"You'll be with me, like a handprint on my heart. And now whatever way our stories end, I know you have re-written mine by being my friend."

– ELPHABA THROPP IN "FOR GOOD" FROM *WICKED*

One Thing Missing

Inspired by "The Moment I Knew" by Taylor Swift

There was one thing missing
>That changed the course of everything
>Remembering the words you said to me
>Unable to shake a feeling of uncertainty
>Something I thought you'd make me feel
>That's why I can't put my faith in you

There was one thing missing
>Pride for everything I've done
>A gleam in the eye
>Seeking out my dreams, full steam ahead
>Seemingly with nothing to lose
>I can't bring myself to that level anymore
>Opposition wins with ease these days
>Nothing can bring me the joy I once had

There was one thing missing
>From day one, I knew you had my back
>Always in my corner
>My partner in crime
>I barely feel you anymore
>Lonely in a world meant for togetherness
>You're here, but distant

There was one thing missing
    Feeling as if time were infinite
    Relentlessly laughing, loving, and living
    It seems we weren't as unbreakable as we thought
    Eventually, I found myself looking back instead of forward
    No one was there for me to lean on or celebrate with
    Destined, now, to only hold you in my heart

There was one thing missing
    How do you find the sun in a rainstorm
    Always struggling to find the light
    Pain around every corner
    Pessimistic to the core
    I tried every trick in the book
    Nothing could fix my broken pieces
    Everything single task became twice as hard
    Some things can't be mended
    Sometimes missing people can't be replaced

There was one thing missing
    You're never prepared to lose someone
    Other people try to fill the void
    Unfortunately, none of them are you

And that was the moment I knew
I had to get used to
Not having you

Shadows

You didn't know the "before you" me
I was doing just fine having nothing
Having no one
Living in the shadows
      Being invisible

Then you came along
Broke down my walls
Convinced me to let you in
Persuaded me to let my guard down
It gave me a taste of something new
      Being seen

Now that you've disappeared
I'm left chasing that unattainable feeling
Living in the shadows

Single

Being alone with myself
           My worst enemy
Makes for some tough days
And I don't want to be *that person*
           Yet I always am
Since I am the single friend
In a friend group of couples

Being an introverted, single twenty-something
In a friend group of couples
Fucking sucks
There is always a time
When you're alone
           And everyone else isn't
It's a shot to your self-esteem
It wears on your self-image
And your inner demons have a field day
About why it's them and not you
           Even though you don't have those kind of feelings

Being an introverted single friend
In a friend group of couples
Fucking sucks
Being constantly surrounded by multiple people
           While craving intimate conversation

You want to speak up
But knowing it won't be the popular opinion
You say you're "okay with anything"
Even when you aren't
    Because you're outnumbered
    And don't want to cause issues
So you create an internal conflict instead
Because everyone had fun
    Except you
And the only one you can blame
    Is you

Being single in your twenties
At Christmastime
Fucking sucks
It's always been my favorite time of year
But it's slowly becoming my least favorite
Because I spend it alone
    Wishing things were different
All I want to do
Is exchange gifts and make memories
But everyone is already doing that
    With other people
    Without me
And it hurts

But I'd never tell them that

Being the single family member
Fucking sucks
Everyone always asks about your love life
      If you're dating
      Why you're not dating
      When you'll start dating
You get defensive about it
Then feel like an asshole for getting upset
Because these are the people you love most
And all they did was take an interest in you
      Which is all you've ever wanted

Sometimes I feel like I'm doing life all wrong
But there are no do-overs
And that fucking sucks

Nothing Left

Do you think I like feeling like this?
Do you think I enjoy saying these things?
I don't.
Actually, I hate it.
But I don't have anything left.
	Nothing to fight for,
	Nothing to fight with.

I ran out of tears a long time ago.
I'm done with the painful part
Now I'm just trying to survive.
To heal
And to move forward.

Lost a Piece of Me

Two years ago he moved away
We did so much together
      Spent all 20 years of my life together
And then he left
I was on my own
I was lost

He barely talks to me
      And that just makes it worse
He always finds a reason
      For me not to visit
What did I do wrong?
Am I that shitty of a person
      That my own brother
      Wants nothing to do with me?

Christmas never feels like Christmas
Without him
I started to lose my spirit

One time my friend joked about it
      How he wasn't talking to me anymore
I knew it was a joke
I even laughed at first
      Then I busted into tears

Lonely

You all have your other people
        Co-workers
        Significant others
        Friends from other places
        Siblings or family
My brother lives almost two hours away
All of my co-workers are at least ten years older
        With families of their own

Is it my fault?
For not letting people in?
I have trust issues
        It's lonely
Other people will break you
And I feel like that's inevitable

I always feared being alone
        Abandoned
Why the hell am I still scared?
I'm already living it

Something's Changed

It used to be necessary
      It was "essential"
I needed to get out of the house
I needed to see other people
I needed to know there were people in my corner
I was in a tough spot
It used to be my favorite part of the week
      The thing that got me through
I didn't mind the drive across town
It was about the company for me

It doesn't do anything for me anymore
It was draining to go
      To pretend I'm having a good time
So why still go?
Because I'm scared
Scared to be alone with my thoughts
Scared to not be surrounded by people
Scared of the questions that inevitably follow
And the answers I may give

Sticks and Stones

High school is as bad as it's going to get
At least that's what I thought
          That's what they all say anyway.
If I told high school me
That I still have room to fall after high school
I wouldn't believe it.

Being bullied
Being talked about
Being laughed at
Being isolated
None of that was fun
But it was just words
Coming from strangers.
The real pain comes in similar ways
          Saying hurtful things
          Invalidating feelings
          Being left out
But it comes from people who know you
          People who knew what hurt you before
          People you trusted
          People you thought loved you.

Words can hurt
But people will never forget
How you made them feel.

They say sticks and stones can break bones
            And they do.
But words?
Words cut deep too
They leave bruises no one can see.

The Hardest Thing

If you are without something for long enough
You get used to it not being there
But the struggle doesn't come from
Deciding not to have it around
The struggle comes in the quiet times
      When it sneaks back in your mind
      When remembering the good times hurts

Some say the hardest thing in life
Is losing someone that you love
I disagree
The hardest thing in life
Is losing someone that you love
      But not losing the love you have for them

Not Enough

People are allowed to change
In fact, there's no preventing it
      We are ever-changing
People, then, are also allowed to change their minds
The person you fall for can turn into a stranger
And you have to decide
      Either to love them anyway
      Or accept that things have changed
      And move on
Neither choice is painless
      And it is no one's fault
Sometimes life leads you to grow apart
Rather than closer together
And sometimes you don't even get a choice
You could fight to love them anyway
      But you'll realize you don't recognize
      What it is you're fighting for
Then you have to accept
That maybe it's not meant to be

You can love someone with everything you've got
And unfortunately
It can still not be enough

Wrong

I've never asked for a lot
And I used to think that was an accomplishment
      I was a low maintenance person
I've learned recently I need to ask for more.

Recently, I have been voicing my needs
      Sharing my feelings
But nothing has been changing.

Maybe I am giving my energy to the wrong people
      How do I find the right ones?
Should I take the time to tell them
Why I feel like they're the wrong people to trust?
      Is it worth it?
If they didn't listen before,
      Why would they start now?

Closing Opened Doors

Why is it so hard for people to stick around?
Why are they constantly mending and breaking my
heart?
Why can't they be there when I need them?
Why can't they be there even when I don't need
them?

I just want to talk to a friend
Say I've been going through a whole lot
  I've been depressed
   Trying to crawl out from rock bottom
It's not a conversation to have over the phone.

One day I finally got the courage
To initiate the conversation.
We'd go to our favorite restaurant
Then get ice cream.
I'd open up about how I'd been feeling
  I needed to.
  I was ready.
Those two things had never lined up before
And that day they did.

But the conversation never happened.

Stepping Stone

Every time I think I've found a place where I belong
The switch gets flipped
And I end up on the outside
Just once I want to be on the inside
I want *one person* to choose me
      One person to make me feel special

I feel like a stepping stone everyone uses
To get where they need to be
Then I get washed away downstream
Like runoff water

Number One

I'm there when you call
I'm there through it all
But when I need you
You have something else to do
I tried to ignore it
Tried longer that I'd care to admit

I'm not competing anymore
I've been down this road before
Life isn't a relay race
But somehow I'm always in second place
I refuse to be anyone but me
      It's the only thing I can be
I'm done being no one's number one
I'm moving on
There's no race to be won
When you are your own number one

I put myself out on the line
With this fragile little heart of mine
Then you threw it down
Stomped it on the ground
I did my part
But you're always coming up short

I want to be needed
I need to be wanted
If that's not something you can be
Then set me free

Unsure

I haven't been writing lately
There isn't much to say
It's been a while since we talked
No progress has been made between us
But I feel lighter

I'm not going to act like I don't miss you
          I do
Call it denial
Call it hope
Part of me doesn't want you to stay gone
Nostalgia finds its way in sometimes
          Seeing an old photo
          Hearing a song
But then it fades away
Just as swift as it appeared

I found some old letters from you
That version of us seems foreign
          Maybe you are
I know I'm different now
          I found my voice and use it

So much time has passed
So much has happened
        Or not happened
We can't just move on
And act like it hasn't
        At least I can't

The Hard Way

Loving someone harder
Won't make them love you more.
You can't make someone love you more.
You can love them as hard as you want
But that won't change their feelings.

I learned that the hard way.

Too Much

I wonder what you're up to
      It kills me not to know
But to get you back
I'd have to open back up
I'd have to let the walls down
I'd have to face my feelings
      And they hurt too much to deal with

Coloring Book

You wrote my name on the front cover
I could hear your voice each time I read it
I worked on it when I missed you
      When I wanted to talk to you
      When I was alone
It took my mind off the spirals
      A safe distraction
Since we were in limbo
Unsure if things would go back to how they were
      But maybe that was my imagination too

It was a gift from you
It is full of all the color missing from my life
And I don't want it anymore
I don't want to be reminded
      Of how alone I am

Dreaming

You were in my dream last night.

It was at a large gathering.
We were on opposite sides of the room
You walked toward me
Grabbed my hand as you passed by
        The way you did when you wanted to talk.
As soon as we were alone
And you opened your mouth to speak
I woke up.

I was nervous.
        What were you going to say?
I was excited.
        Our long silence will be broken.
        I missed your voice.
I was mad.
        It wasn't real.
        But it felt so real.
I wish I had never woken up.

They say when you dream of someone
It means that person misses you.
I wonder if there's any chance
You really do miss me too.

Someone Once Said

Just didn't want you thinking I don't think about
you everyday
You are my number one, baby
You're my world
I'll love you forever
I'm so proud of you
My distance doesn't change that
I promise I'm not neglecting you
Never a burden to me
I met you for a reason
I don't deserve you
It's beautiful, like you
I love every part of you
My love
We both suffer. We will always understand. We will
never judge.
I can't wait to see you
Your heart shines
Thank you for being my best friend
There will never be a day I'm not thankful for you
That's all I want, for you to be happy
Always your girl
Being your best friend is my greatest achievement
You will always be my favorite hello and a goodbye I
hopefully never have to say

I cherish you
I miss you every day
All my love
Love of my life
You fill me with love each and every day
I cannot wait until we never have to part again
You honestly are one of the purest hearts I will and
have ever met
You are a gift to this world
Never ever ever think you have to live your life alone
I can't express enough how much I adore you
No one will live up to you
You're the gift that keeps on giving
Words don't seem to do you justice
I just wanted to spend some time with you
I haven't seen your face today, I love you
You take care of me so well
You are one of the few people I know that makes all
my worries silent
I don't know what I did to deserve you
You have changed my life

I wish I was there for you
Me too
I don't want you to feel like you're less than
Too late
You are everything and more, I couldn't imagine a
life without you
Look around
You came into my life when I needed you most
One of the most terrifying thoughts I've had
Is that our time is up

Time Changes Things

Everything changed the day you came into my life
Now that you're gone, they changed again

"I feel seen" became
          "I'm invisible again"
"I trust you" became
          "You let me down"
"We laughed until we cried" became
          "I cried myself to sleep"
"I've never felt so loved" became
          "I've never felt more alone"
"I miss you" became
          "A weight has been lifted"
"I love you" became
          "I love you but"
"Dear moments" became
          "Distant memories"
"Best friend" became
          "Stranger"
"Hold on" became
          "Let go"

I let my guard down
But now my walls are higher than ever
We had so many plans

That will drift away in the wind
We were so close
Now you feel a million miles away
You said you needed space
I just want you to come back
I thought it was forever
But maybe it was never meant to be

People in my life use a revolving door
I just thought you'd stay a while longer

Fiction

They say writers write what they know
I may not know what it's like to have a good friend
But I do know what I want from one

When it comes to friendships
Writing characters is my wishful thinking
But in the end
      It's all fiction

Fine

We all bend the truth
Especially when it feels like our armor

I try not to lie often
Just enough to keep the peace
      To keep others from looking too closely
"I'm fine" is my most frequent and loyal safeguard
I use it as a shield to hold the frontlines
      A bandage I continue to reapply

I choose the path that hides my heart
Because once you open up
I've found that people don't know what to do with it
They worry
They feel sorry for you
Or they treat you like a problem to solve

The truth can be heavy
Sometimes too heavy to hand to someone else
So I will stand my ground
Brandishing my spoken shield:
      "I'm fine"
And carry it on my own
Bracing for impact

Fade Out

The flames burned bright
And spread with every gust of the wind.
Hot to the touch
Glowing through the night
Everything in sight was fuel to the fire.

Then came the rain.
The sizzle and the smoke
Yet a small ember remained.
Though it was a slow burn
An occasional breeze would rekindle it
        Brief as it may be.

Maybe I always knew
The fire would eventually go out.

Heartbeats and a Held Breath

"Ever feel like you're breathing underwater, and you have to stop because you're gulping in too much fluid?"

– NICK ANDREAS IN *BREATHING UNDERWATER*

BY ALEX FLINN

Obscurity

My eyes are open,
        But I cannot see.
My brain is a hive,
        Missing its queen bee.
Perhaps it's a ghost town
        With a lone ranger in the square.
Or a single evergreen tree
        While the rest of the forest is bare.

I'm not sure if I'm isolated
Overworked
Depressed
Lost
Stressed
All I know is my eyes are open
And there is a fog
In front of me.

Emotion Blind

Happiness feels forced
Nothing can just put a smile on my face
        I force it there
But it never stays
Just as quickly as I flash it
        It fades away

I don't trust people
Their words carry no weight in my heart
All I want is to be loved
But I constantly feel nothing
I'm told that I am loved
So why can't I fucking feel it?
        I just want to feel something
I'm not even depressed
        How pathetic is that?
I'm not miserable enough to be depressed
I don't want to give up
        I love living too much
I'm actually terrified of death
The earliest I can remember having panic attacks
        They were about the fear of death
        The fear of no longer being alive
I am hopelessly stuck in the middle
I'm forcing myself to be content

With living unhappily, living unfulfilled
Am I even capable of feeling happy?
      Would I recognize it if I felt it?
Am I longing for something I've never felt?
I could be waiting a lifetime to find it
When you fake something for so long
It becomes the truth
But convincing myself that I'm happy isn't working
I feel like I'm emotion blind
I can't tell if I've felt so much
      That I feel nothing at all
Or if I'm just unable to feel
I want to be better
I want help
But I have to ask for it
      That's where the problem lies

Running Low

I am exhausted as soon as I wake up
I am wide awake as I lay down at night
I'm not excited about my own accomplishments
          In fact, I wish I hadn't achieved them
I am not motivated
I need a change
But I don't care enough to take action
My chest feels like it is carrying a mountain
          Have you ever seen anything move a mountain?
          Me either
I look back at old pictures and videos
And barely recognize the person I see
I look forward to time by myself
But I hate being alone
I work so that I can do things I want
          Things that bring me joy
But I don't even know what those things are anymore
I feel like I'm constantly on the verge of crying
But I don't let myself
          Even though I want to
In the moment I am a coward
          I don't stand up for myself
          I lie for their comfort
          Instead of standing up for my sanity

Prepare to endure the verbal beatdown of internal
conflict
      You'll never be loved by anyone
      Look at you, why would anyone find you
      attractive?
      You're broken
      Get used to being alone
      You're a fraud
Believe it or not
These are the nice ones

I actively avoid mirrors
      I can't stand the sight of myself
I'm quiet because the sound of my voice
      Nauseates me
My cheeks are chubby
I have no self confidence
My body aches
My heart is full of love
      But no one to give it to
It is meaningless
I live in a cycle
It is driving me deeper into this hole
I'm too far down to climb out
I'm too weak to fight back

If this is how life is supposed to be
    I don't want it
I want to be able to treasure it
Look at myself in the mirror
Have confidence in my thoughts and words
Be secure in being unique
Listen to my favorite songs without crying
Confide in my friends when I need help

Smile

I'm tired of crying
I'm tired of pain
I'm tired of heartache
I'm tired of having to convince myself
    I'm worth all this trouble
My tank is on "E"
With happiness sputtering out in specks
Soon I will run out
    What will I do then?

Fears

I am always hesitant to say
How I am really feeling
I fear that if I'm honest
I'll get abandoned again
Once I tell someone the truth
  It's hard to tell if they genuinely care
  Or if they're changing just because I spoke up
I'm afraid if I step back
It's just another reason for them to leave me out

I feel so isolated lately
And I don't know if I can bear
  Losing one more person

Incapable

How bold of me to assume
That the people in my life know me.

One thing is for sure
Next time they when they ask what I want
        I will say "nothing"
And it will not be a humble or cliché response.
It's because what I really want
Is something I know you're incapable of giving.

Push-Over

I am always put on the back burner
       But I can only blame myself
I love on my people
       I give the impression that I'll always love them
Even if that means putting myself second
And as true as that may be
That doesn't make it okay
       Or make it hurt any less
When they push me to the side

Tumbleweed

Something has changed
I've been trying to figure it out for months
But maybe what we had before
Is just gone forever

I don't know what's good for me anymore
Which way is up, and which is down?
I need to talk about it, but I don't want to
     Even if I did, where would I start?
I feel like I'm going through the motions of life
     A shell of myself
     Numb
     Blowing in the wind
I need to be me again
I miss me
     I don't like this version

Numb

I've heard people say,
"It's better to hurt than feel nothing at all"
And I am so over that fucking saying
I took in so much hurt
   And hurt
   And hurt
I kept thinking, *how can this pain possibly be better?*

I've endured because I thought I was supposed to
But all I have to show for it are scars

I've poured out so much
Without getting anything in return
   That my well has run dry
I have nothing left to give anymore

Give me the numb
Give me the nothing
I can't take the pain anymore

The hurt is supposed to be
What reminds me I'm alive
Yet it is the very thing killing me

Dishonest

I spend a lot of time lying
Most often to myself
I didn't let myself feel anything
That was the slightest deviation from "okay"
>No pain
>No joy
>No sorrow

Kind of skating by
I said I was a shell of myself
The scary part was people bought it
>Hell, I bought it

I convinced myself I was still me
Yet I was avoiding all the things that made me feel
I was always battling the idea
That I did something wrong
>Drove people away
>Said too much
>Said too little
>Hurt people

And that caused me a lot of pain
>The real pain came in the not knowing

Sometimes I look at the pictures in my room
>Reread the notes
>Relive the memories

Watch the videos
They give me some comfort
Make me smile when I forget how to
But most of the time I look at them
I feel sad because
I realize I don't smile that big anymore

In December, I moved to my brother's old bedroom
I told everyone a different excuse
The real reason was because I missed him
And some nights I couldn't bear to be in my room
        Seeing the smiles I can't produce anymore
        Feeling the warmth of hugs I don't get anymore
It's overwhelming
But I don't have the heart to take them down
And admit it's all different now

So here I am
Unable to be honest with anyone
        Including myself
About how I'm feeling
Except for on a piece of paper
Why is this so hard for me?

If It Ain't Broke,
Don't Fix It

My mental spirals always end at the same place
   I'm going to be alone forever
I'm a little disappointed
Over time, I thought my anxiety
Would get more creative
   More original
My panic over being alone my whole life
Is getting old

At least my brain understands
Not to give up on a tactic
That still works

Island

I feel like I'm on an island.
I feel like I'm all on my own.
I know I have people who care about me,
      People that love me.

I feel like I have people,
But I feel like they don't have me.
I don't feel them.
I can't make myself feel them.

Puzzle

There isn't one person in my life
That knows everything about me.
I only give away bits and pieces of myself
      Different pieces to different people.
Everyone has a piece of the puzzle
And I choose them strategically.

I've never felt secure enough
To give someone the whole picture.
I think only a few souls deserve the kind of love
That hands them your heart
      As well as the power to shatter it to pieces.
Maybe that's why I always feel incomplete
      Unfulfilled
      Unfinished.

Shooting Star

I wish I had friends looking out for me
To tell me "This is a bad idea"
To tell me they are proud of me
To support my dreams
To celebrate my accomplishments
To accept my shortcomings
To wipe my tears when I cry
To guide me through hard times
      Show me the light
Or something as simple as
      To have someone to share my day with

Maybe Someday

Everyone has someone else but me
Some have a boyfriend or girlfriend
Some live far away
Some don't have a single thing to say
Some have a friend they'd rather be with anyway
Some I can't trust
Some aren't close enough for me to open up to
Some I'm unsure about
      One day things were just different
Some said they'd come back
      But I'm still waiting

So I'll just lay here
Crying myself to sleep
Wishing things were different
Wishing I had someone with me
      To ease some of the pain
And until that day comes
I'll be wishing and waiting for someday

How Did This Happen?

How did I get here?
How did my smiles turn into frowns?
How did belly laughs turn into muffled sobs?
How did joy turn into depression?
How did plans every night turn into loneliness?
How did I go from belonging to feeling so lost?
How did it get so bad?
How did this happen?
How did I lose control?
How did I lose myself?
How did I lose everyone else?
How do I make it stop?
How do I get out?
How do I go on?

How did I get here?
And why does it keep happening?

Why do all roads lead me to rock bottom?

The Carousel Keeps Turning

Inspired by *Grey's Anatomy*

I lay awake at night
Listening to the white noise of my fan
Watching the blades rotate
I'm wide awake
  Just the darkness and I
I contemplate doing something productive
But I don't want to get out of bed
My mind is going a mile a minute
  Anticipating
  Wishing
  Longing
  Worrying
  Hating
Maybe if I lay with my eyes closed long enough
  I'll drift to sleep
But no luck
The off switch in my brain
Has been broken for years
  I can always hear the voice
  I vividly remember every single dream
  I feel the excruciating weight of every emotion
It is exhausting

Soon I wake up
>More tired than when I went to sleep
Still unmotivated
I drag my feet till I reach the bathroom
>I prefer to be in the dark
>So I don't have to see myself
I brush my teeth
Put in my contacts
I splash my face with water then leave
I sip my coffee and nibble on breakfast
>Debate with myself about returning to bed
>Although I know I can't
I go to work
>I put on my mask
Answering calls with my customer service voice
Professionally replying to emails
>Scanning barcodes
>Stocking shelves
>Placing orders
When the clock strikes four, I punch out
As soon as I leave the building
I can finally lower my mask

I head home
I talk myself into a basic human activity
>Walking
After a long exhausting day at work
The last thing I want is to talk to people
I stick my headphones in and go on a stroll
For a brief time, I'm on the verge of peace
>The sun is setting
>There is a slight breeze
>Interaction is not expected from a passerby
>All I can hear is my music
>And I'm surrounded by nature

Unfortunately, all good things come to an end
>I am back home
I clean up and make some dinner
When I hear my parents get home
The mask returns
>I'm exhausted
And as soon as my head hits the pillow
I'm wide awake

And the carousel just keeps on turning

High Definition

Sometimes I like to just sit in silence
If I sit long enough
I can hear faint echoes of the past
If I look at a picture
And close my eyes
I can feel the day happening around us
       The weather
       The sounds
       The smells
       The emotions
I captured every moment in HD
Tucked away for a rainy day

But I'm enduring a hurricane
And those moments just cause me more pain

Flip the Hourglass

Do you ever stop and think
About all the things you could have missed
If you had given up when you wanted to?

I wanted to give up once before
        Maybe more than once
And if I would have
I would have never met you.

Here I am
        Back on the edge
Wondering if someone will show up this time
To remind me and make me believe yet again
        That life is worth living.

Are they coming soon?
I sure hope so.

Thief of Comparison

It may be fair to claim
I love all of them way too much
I am aware of it
      But I can't help it
I'll never be able to explain
How much they mean to me
And no matter how hard they try
I know they can't love me
      As much as I love them

I can't wait to watch them
      Smile ear to ear
      Laugh as hard as they've ever laughed
      Fall in love
      Walk down the aisle
      Start a family
      Succeed
      Get the promotion
      Realize their dreams

My biggest fear is that
I will not be there to witness it
They are the best people I know
Destined for greatness
      They're already halfway there
So why the hell haven't they
      Left me in the dust?

Weight

All I have to offer is weight
An anchor to keep them where they are
      I drag them down with me
I float from person to person
Being their personal progressional speed bump
      Slowing them down
With no roots
No wings
No reason

For You

I was living for the people around me
Living so I'm not the one to cause them pain
At that point, living for me wasn't enough
Honestly, I didn't want to live
          I couldn't see a point in it
I couldn't find my purpose
I often thought there wasn't one for me to find
But I didn't necessarily want to die either
My main motivation to keep going
Was that I didn't want to not be the reason
          That my loved ones hurt
          Cried
          Longed
That motivation carried more weight than my will
To simply live for myself

I want the best for my people
Regardless of the price I have to pay to get it

Little did they know
That when I said I'd die for them
    I meant every word
    Every time
Little did they know
When they would tell me they love me
And my response was always "I love you more"
    It was because I did.
The only reason I was there
    And I'm still here
Was because I love them more than I love myself

And I hope they know I always will love them

Why I Can't Breathe

I went downstairs and I knew something was up
My parents weren't as excited to go as me
My uncle was having trouble breathing
        He told them not to call for help
"Momma Momma" he called
He didn't recognize Grandma was sitting next to
him
        Holding his hand
        Wiping his tears
        And wiping her own
Dad didn't want to see him that way
        So he stayed with us
He likes it when I am the DJ of the road trip
        I still remember the song that was playing
        I haven't listened to it since
When he hung up the phone
He told me that my uncle had passed away
A single tear slid underneath the lens of his sun-
glasses
It was enough to break my heart
"I could feel it; his soul leaving the Earth"
I'll never forget hearing my grandma's cries as the
casket closed
It's cliché but parents should never have to bury
their kids

I took a deep breath, but when I exhaled
More tears came out than air

A buddy of mine
Fought cancer his whole life
        Fought harder than anyone I knew
Near the end, it took advantage of his weaknesses
Seizure after seizure, it never ended
Once they took him into surgery
He never woke back up
        Just like that he was gone
Any death is traumatic
But the death of a child is unimaginable pain
        It shouldn't be allowed to happen
        A kid dying from cancer
I held my breath
        I couldn't start crying
        Because I knew I'd never stop
I had to be strong

Mom texted "I think Dad had a stroke"
        My heart stopped
        My stomach dropped
        My worst nightmare was realized
Mom insisted he needed to get checked
He insisted he was okay
I got a text message
        Two hundred and fifty-eight over one hun-

dred and twelve
     His blood pressure upon hospital admission
     Not a typo
From then on, every text made me anxious
Thinking it'd be bad news
It took him months to recover
     He still isn't fully recovered
Lots of hospital visits, physical therapy, and changes
He took baby steps toward "better"
My brother and I talked about it
     How everything felt different
We weren't sure why, but everything had changed

These days I often catch myself holding my breath
Other people have noticed as well
I feel like if I exhale
     I'll cry
     I'll lose it
     I'll never catch my breath
Even when days are going well
I still get scared to breathe

It was December 17th, 2017
I got a message that he passed away
"He loved you so much"
"You were his favorite"
He was like a second father to me
     My number one fan

And now he's gone
I began to sob
      Maybe it was the meds
      Maybe it was the pain I was already in
I couldn't stop
Get it together, catch your breath

It was the first day of workouts
Senior year
I knew I was out of shape, but damn
What the hell
There are hives all over
"Let's go up to the showers"
"I'll make sure no one comes in"
I looked up and all I could see were rainbow dots
Then it hit me
I felt my way to the door and cracked it open
I say, weak and out of breath
      "I can't breathe"
Darkness
When I open my eyes, I'm on the floor
More darkness
I open my eyes again, I'm in an ambulance
The tips of my fingers were purple
My blood pressure was 58/12
Darkness again
I'm in an ER covered in tubes
My mom took me home to get tests

From then on
Every new place
Every bite of food
Every allergy test
Even when I returned to school
        It made me hold my breath
        Bracing myself for the worst
        Bracing for the world to go dark again

It had gone up and down
        Her health that is
She had a risky surgery
I was nervous all day
"It's good news, she's awake and recovering"
Sixteen days later, she passed
We went up north for the ceremony
        "You're the granddaughter with a book"
        "She was so proud of you"
        "She said it was incredible"
A brief smirk flashed
Although I didn't feel like smiling
I knew if I exhaled, I'd lose it
        I wish it were her saying it to me
Every time I hear about it
        I wish it were her words
        Her voice

Easter she was admitted to the hospital
        Put on a ventilator
        Denied for a lung transplant
"A good morning, alert and responding"
"Steady and strong"
Five days later, the lung collapsed
Fifty minutes later, so did the other one
Later that evening, she joined the angels
I cried, then gathered myself
Then cried again
I went to work and brought my shallow breaths
Careful not to think too much
        Or to breathe too deep
I held it all in
And let it all out the second I got home
Exhale

"Fly high"

Tainted

Is it possible for a day to be both
One of the best days
And one of the saddest?

Grandma was the one who started it all
She introduced me to the love of my life
      Reading
      Writing
      Storytelling
She sent me a magical story
      Having no idea how impactful it would be
It inspired me to want to be an author
To help people escape their reality by reading a book
She was an educator
      Just like my mom
      Just like me

I had always wanted to be a writer
I dreamed about it forever
For a while I worked in secret
      I still do sometimes
But I was always "practicing my craft"
      Carrying a pen and notepad everywhere
      As if it were my magic wand
Creating characters in my head

Giving them names and backstories
Thinking of what they'd look like
How they'd dress
Talking to them as if they were real
      Looking insane along the way

I was nervous
Grandma wasn't doing well
She needed surgery
      A dangerous surgery for her state
They told us she may not make it through
So they kept pushing it back
In hopes it would give her a better shot
      At waking back up
      At surviving
One day she told them to stop moving it
      She signed a DNR
      Do not resuscitate
She said either He will take me, or He won't
      We prayed that it wasn't a sign of her giving up

After many years of work and editing
I had written a complete manuscript
I had agreed to terms with a New York Publisher
      I was an author
      Well, almost
We had a cover
We had most of the edits

Then the COVID-19 pandemic halted everything
    And I mean everything

I sent Grandma the printed-out manuscript
    I wanted her to at least see that I'd done it
    I finished!
    Just in case the surgery didn't go well
She received it and started the day before surgery
    "I can't wait to finish it"
But we were already making arrangements
    Alternate Christmas possibilities
    Travel plans
    Work arrangements
Preparing for the worst
But praying for a miracle
    And we got one
A successful surgery
    She made it!
Thank God
We were able to exhale
    For a little while at least
She prevailed nonetheless
She read the whole manuscript
    "Enjoyed the book"
    "Send another"
    It was a big deal since Grandma never texted

The publisher needed my final proof
Battlefield was finalized, printed, and shipped
		Delivered on December 27, 2020
I signed one and mailed it to Grandma right away
		A belated Christmas gift
I got to give one to my brother, Mom, and Dad
I gifted them to my friends
I got to announce it to the world
That I was going to be an author
		Officially
		Finally!!
I was still in shock
		Speechless
I had a release date
		January 8th, 2021

Grandma never said anything about receiving it
		I figured she'd at least call my mom
The day after it was delivered, we got the news
She had passed away that morning
My aunt said my package was in her room
		Opened
She saw it!
She read what I wrote to her in it
"Dreams really do come true
And I've been dreaming this one my whole life.
It is my greatest pleasure to gift you my first novel

Hopefully the first of many!
Enjoy! Love Darah"
My aunt gave me the book back
I decided to let the funeral director lay it with her
      She had to show Grandpa
The first day of funeral services was January 8th,
2021
      Release day

So is it possible
For one of the best days of your life
And one of the saddest days of your life
To be the same?
No
No matter how hard I try to celebrate
      Be excited that my dream came true
I feel that grief
      The loss
      The pain
      The sadness
These two big life moments
Forever intertwined in my story
Painting happy memories
In hues of blue

I Still Talk To You When It's Quiet

"The ones who love us never really leave us."
– SIRIUS BLACK IN *HARRY POTTER AND THE PRISONER OF AZKABAN* BY J.K. ROWLING

Stages of Grief

I can't say anything right now
It still doesn't feel real
I can see everything I want to say
But the thoughts zoom by too fast
  Kind of like life
I'm grasping at straws
I thought I was getting through
  It turns out I'm still going through
It wasn't the end of the storm
  Just the eye of the hurricane
I can't handle another wave of this
I'm drowning in the impact zone
I'm going down like the Titanic
  Without a lifeboat in sight

I want to say something
I want to tell everyone
  How much you meant to me
  How much I loved you
  How glad I am that you're family
It doesn't seem fair that you got to see
So much of me
And I barely got to see you
You've known me my whole life

I have no idea what life's like without you
        I guess I'll have to learn now
It's not fair

It's eleven eighteen at night
Three days ago they said you were
        "Stable and strong"
Now they're telling me
You're gone
What the fuck
I wish I believed in the afterlife
        A place after this
Because I really want to see you again
But I think a lot of that is bullshit
        To ease people's pain
Fuck another life
I want more time in this one
I don't want to have to search
For you again
        I already had you

I feel so much
I still have so much to say
So much left to do
        Together

Please don't make me do them without you
Please don't make me see them without you
Please let me tell you
Please don't leave us here
Please don't go

I never thought I'd have to say goodbye
So soon
I'm not ready for it
No more jokes
No more surprises
No more trips
How was I supposed to know
The last time was the last time
      The last smile
      The last hug
      The last moment with you
Hold tight to your people

I miss you so much

No More

No more intercepting Mom's phone
            When I see your name on the caller ID
Then she says she can't find her phone
Because she thinks I am talking to you on mine

No more Texas A&M shirts everywhere we go
No more "Where are you guys going next?"
            Followed by an "oh fun, take me with you"
No more going through three pots of coffee every
morning
No more endless questions about my next book
No more big, long hugs
No more seeing you
            Only more tears

Party's Over

Today I realized
That for the first time
I won't be able to talk to you on your birthday

I'd normally send you the minions
        Wearing party hats
        And blowing party horns
You sent them to me first
You thought they were funny and cute
I knew whenever I'd send them
        They'd make you smile

Now I can't send them
Because you aren't here anymore
And I hate that

God, I miss you

Coping

It was never fair that you left us so soon
You made each day brighter
You made each smile bigger
You made each laugh louder
You were a light
        All I see now is darkness

Peering through windows from the outside
Staring at screens rather than at each other
Deprived of closeness
Forced to distance
        Comfort doesn't work in isolation

I should have gotten to say goodbye
I should have gotten one last hug
        One last kiss on the forehead
        One last conversation
Everything changed so fast
One minute you were stable
And the next you were gone

I hope you weren't in pain
I hope you weren't scared

I hope you knew you were loved
        I love you
I hope you knew we'd eventually be okay
        You are so missed
I hope you knew we'd always talk like you're still in
the room
I hope you can still laugh at our jokes
And reminisce on our many memories
        Wherever you are
I hope my heart stops breaking
        Every time I think of you
And I hope I can always feel your warmth
        From the memories I am holding on to

You Were Back

I had a dream that you were back
Standing in front of me
Wearing your favorite Aggies shirt
        I cried
You were back!

I got to feel your hug again
Hear your voice again
Tell you everything I didn't get to say
Introduce you to all the people in my life
I got to laugh with you again
        My favorite thing to do

I had a dream you were back
        Damn it felt so good
But I began to hear
The faint ringing of an alarm
"No, no, no, no, no!"
I pleaded as it all melted away

I opened my eyes
You were still gone
I had a dream
It was just a dream, though.
        Too good to be true

Heaven's Doors

There isn't a day that goes by
That I don't look up at the sky
Days turn into weeks and weeks into years
But no amount of time can slow my tears
Into the future, I don't want to go
A world without you, I don't want to know
It feels like the walls are caving in
I want to escape but I am locked in
You're soaring like a dove
Leaving behind all the ones you love

I can see all the sunshine
But I'm drowning in the rain
There should be a flood warning
For all this pain
I can't simply move on
Knowing that you're gone

Into paradise, may the angels lead you
Rest in peace, go on your way
I hope that I get my wings like you got yours
And someday when I get to see you again
You'll be welcoming me into heaven's doors

Cardinals on the Patio

I thought it was a myth
Something people created to give them comfort
Yet I never saw cardinals around
Until I lost you

He just appeared on our patio furniture
      The day we got back from saying goodbye to him
I watched him through the glass door
We made eye contact, he chirped, and flew away
A few years later, I noticed he was back
      And shortly followed by another
It couldn't have been a coincidence
That I had just lost another person

The cycle continued
And as I lost people
      We'd gain a new little red bird

I will never forget about you all
      I never could
But I never remember how much I miss you
Until days like today
      When I see four cardinals on the patio

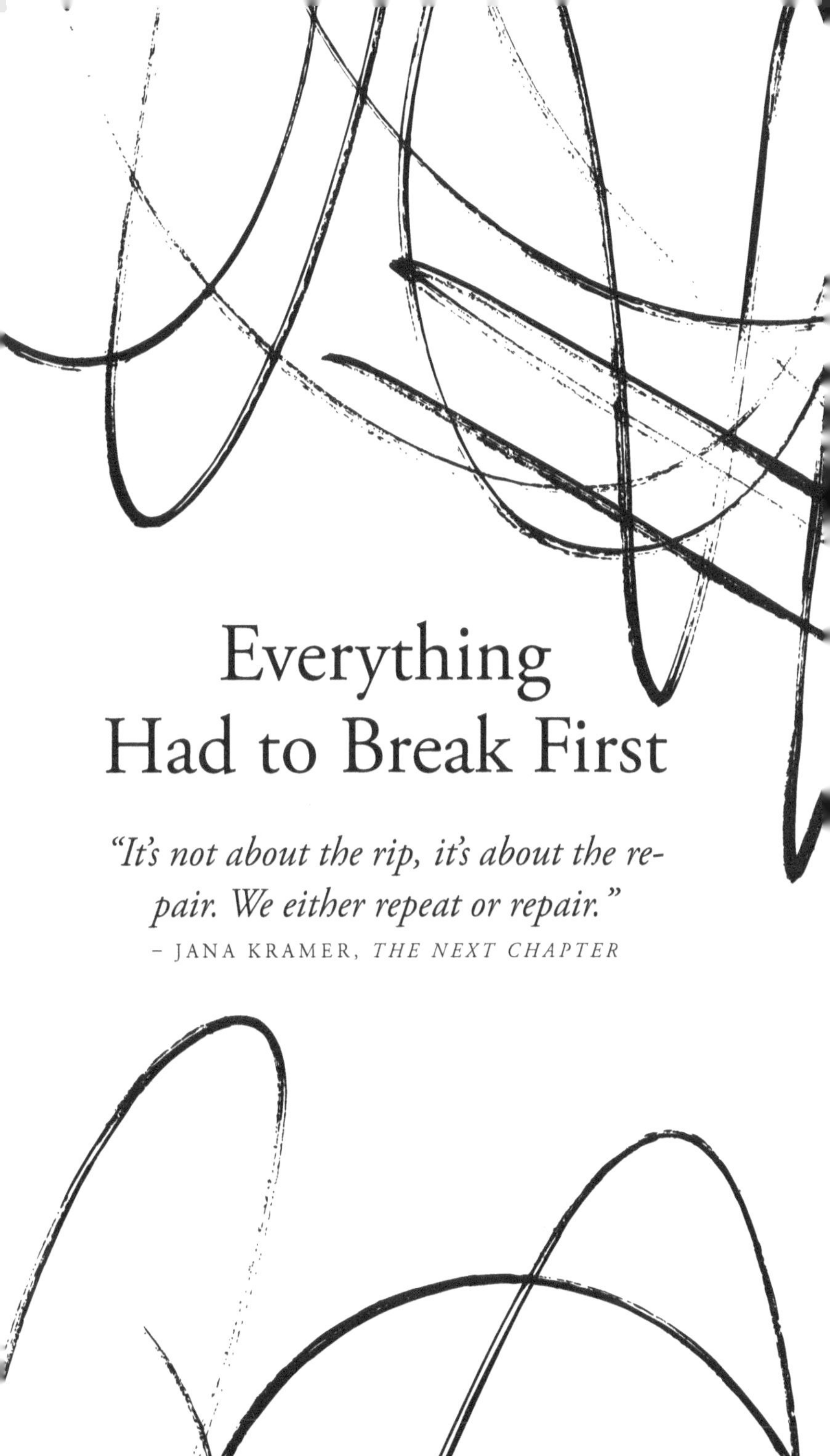

Everything Had to Break First

"It's not about the rip, it's about the re-pair. We either repeat or repair."
– JANA KRAMER, *THE NEXT CHAPTER*

Living the Dream

People always say that
Going to college
       Your twenties
Are the best time of your life
I wish they'd stop saying that
People like me will expect it
Then find out that time in your life fucking sucks

You have to schedule time with friends
       Otherwise forget seeing them
You have expenses
You work to make a living
But don't get to spend it on what you want
Everyone is in different stages of life
Some are single
Some are engaged
Some are married
Some have kids
Not to mention there was a pandemic
       Nine months after my college graduation
We were forced to communicate virtually
       Mandated to distance ourselves

Your late teens and twenties are fucking hard
You're trying to figure out who you are
Trying to establish yourself
Just trying to stay afloat
Learning personal and professional limits
Setting boundaries while learning how to set boundaries
Balancing work, family, friends, and mental health
Nobody warned us about this
        At least I wasn't warned
I was thrown a massive curveball
And I'm holding on for dear life
Waiting for the good part
Begging for it all to click into place

But hey, at least "You're still young"
        Right?
"We have all the time in the world"
        Right?

Careless

You know when you get sick
And you say you'd do anything
To feel normal again
Or that you'd never take health for granted again
Then you get better
      And get careless almost immediately
Why do we do that?
Why can't we just remember
      To value the little things

You can beg the universe to give you what you want
Then once you get it
You fuck it up

Heartburn

I often think of that warm August night
When we were endless in the summer moonlight
Sparks danced every direction that I turned
But it was just fuel to the fire where my heart
burned

I was too strong to cry
But too weak to hold on or ask you to stay
Trying my damnedest to keep the floodgates at bay

Although I was too broken not to
I tried not to fall apart
But Band-Aids and glue can't fix a broken heart

I thought love would save me
Yet it swallowed me whole
And the darkness will keep
The light that you stole

I thought **your** love would save me
Instead I had to learn
Not every flame brings love, you see
Some just end with heartburn

My Own Hero

People come and go
But you can never leave yourself
          My fatal flaw
I'm the only guaranteed constant in my life
If I'm unstable
How do I expect my life and relationships to be a
solid foundation?

My stability is my responsibility
I can lean on others
But at the end of the day
No one is going to rescue me
          Except me

I have to decide to be better
Rather than waiting for someone to do it for me

Leaving

I want it so bad
But I don't want to leave
      Everything I've ever known
Anyone who starts over is scared
      Of change
      Of failure
      Of the new
It's not going to be easy
I'm not good at letting go
But the fact is I'm choosing a new path
I'm choosing to leave
      Choosing to isolate myself
I'm the one making the move
Which makes it that much worse
Because I only have myself to blame

Choices

I used to think
My biggest fear was being alone
But what I'm really scared of
Is enjoying being alone
       Or being comfortable being alone

I don't like the feeling of missing someone
And if I make the decision to be alone
I'm choosing to live in a feeling that I hate
Yet at the same time
       I am choosing peace

It's an oxymoron
       Or juxtaposition
And I don't know what to do
Can I have both?
       Can you have both discomfort and peace?

Outgrown

They don't need me anymore
        Maybe there was a time that they did
        Maybe I made it up
But I'm scared of moving on
        Letting go
I'm scared I'm no longer needed
The only one who needs me is me
I have never learned or practiced being there for myself
This is my chance
        To spread my wings

Charlotte will always be my home
But for the first time ever
I tried to choose me
All of my reasons for staying
Involve other people
        People who barely speak to me
But I don't want to let go
I am comfortable
But being comfortable is not living
Being comfortable means I'm not growing

I have to move forward
I have to give myself room to progress
Because everything I've known
I've outgrown

Falling on My Sword

Growing up, my biggest conflicts were external
      I was made fun of
      I was lied to
I became scared of being vulnerable
      Of my true heart or true self being exposed
Because when those delicate pieces get broken
They are the hardest to mend

Friends and family tried to rescue me from my
thoughts
They would tell me time after time
That they loved me
That they were telling me the truth
That I could trust them
      But how could I?
That would require me to let them see me
Which could only cause more pain
      Right?
That drove them away
Because you can only repeat yourself so many times
Before you grow tired of not being heard

In an effort to protect myself from the world
I retreated into myself and the people I already
knew
I claimed it was all I needed
        That was a lie –
In turn, I was introduced to a new, worse pain
An enemy I can never escape
        Myself
And all my conflicts became internal
The outside world couldn't hurt me anymore
Hell, I didn't even give it the chance to

My positive thoughts always leave me feeling uneasy
But when the negative thoughts roll in
        I have no problem taking them to heart
Why is it so easy to believe the bad things?
My happiness is my responsibility
        And mine alone
And believing the lies I feed myself
Is something I need to unlearn

Gotta Start Somewhere

Once I thought I couldn't feel
I thought that since I'd felt so much
      All at once
I couldn't feel at all anymore
Neither of which were true

I thought something was wrong with me
I thought I needed help
      And I did need help
I need to stand up for myself
Do what I need to do for me
I need to get to know myself
So I can trust myself
      Love myself
That's where I will start
That is a solid foundation
      That I can build on

I can feel
I am capable of everything I've been looking for
I just haven't found it
And that is okay

Lessons I Learned Along the Way

"We run from joy because we don't think we deserve happiness, but it's a package deal. There is no joy without pain."

—MEREDITH GREY, GREY'S ANATOMY

The Game of Life

I did it almost everyday
When I did it for me, it was fun.
I used to love it, you know?
I used to do it to escape
      Escape from the pressure
      Escape from myself
      Escape from reality

But one day something changed.

The game became a job
The clock was not on my side
I had lost all my passion
And I was merely along for the ride.

It paid the bills.
      It got me through
But I longed for it to end.
Because I knew the day the ball stops bouncing,
Is the day my new life begins.

I found something new inside of me
Something that kickstarts my heart
      Something that puts a smile on my face
And I'll get to do it one day.
      You'll see
Just wait till the ball stops bouncing.

Without

Loss is necessary
If we had everything we needed
There'd be no striving
Life would be mundane and meaningless
Loss creates value

Without space
        You don't know the value of closeness
Without death
        We couldn't fathom how lucky we are to live
Without sadness
        We wouldn't feel the warmth of joy
Without failure
        Success isn't as sweet
Without losing
        Winning seems normal
Without sickness
        We can't see the blessing of health
Without pain
        Pleasure is nothing new
Without ordinary
        There is no extraordinary

Obstacles and challenges add flavor to our everyday

lives
Don't wish away what makes your life
    Exceptional
    Unique
    Worth living

Chances

Be okay with brokenness
It's okay to cry
It's okay to have bad days
      Weeks
      Months
      Years
It's okay to not feel whole
It's okay to feel like you don't belong

It's okay to not know what to do
Or not know what comes next
As long as through the lows
We learn
We grow
We keep taking steps forward
      Even if there's resistance
      Even if there's difficulty
      Even if there's hesitation
      Even if there's anxiety
Brokenness breeds growth

So when you fall
Get back up
You owe yourself as many chances
        If not more
        Than you give
To everyone else

One Day

I break promises to myself so easily
But keep my word to those who hurt me
I pour into other people plenty
But my cup always remains empty
By everyone else, I am quickly impressed
But when I look in the mirror, all I see is a mess

How is everyone else able to fly and be free
While I'm digging for an opportunity
Why am I your crutch when you'd let me fall
It's like you don't care about me at all
Why do I always find myself in a bind
Why can't I hush the negativity in my mind
Why do I always let myself be defined
By people who'd be better left behind
I lift them up despite their behavior
Yet the moment I fuck up, I'm a failure
I'm on my own when my strength begins to waiver
And when they need me, I play the savior

One of these days I'll learn to rise above
One of these days I'll find a way to laugh and love
One of these days I'll be fully healed
One of these days it will be revealed
That I will no longer need a shield
In this life that is a battlefield

One of these days I will stop holding back
I'll have my life on track
I'll have a plan of attack
I'll be on the come up, so don't call it a comeback
I'll see the life I've always planned
I'll hold my future in the palm of my hand
Instead of leaning, I'll be able to stand

One day all the work I've done will be on display
And it will not matter what they have to say
And I only pray that on that day
I'll have cleared all the obstacles
And done everything possible
To live in a mindset most optimal
To make the doubters inaudible
To achieve the impossible
And make all of my dreams proximal
Holdfast that succeeding is not optional
On that day, I'll be unstoppable

We Make Our Own

Hard work beats talent
When talent doesn't work hard
And life can get you down
When it catches you off guard
Nothing is ever handed to you
You must work for what you have
Money doesn't grow on trees
And no one clears your path
To find peace, you must leave hate behind
There is no positive life with a negative mind
The grass isn't greener on the other side
Your side is dying because you never tried
Happiness is not a destination
It's a state of mind
When the sky is a cloudy gray
You need to bring your own sunshine
We create opportunities
From the choices that we make
It's only the rest of our lives
Which means there's a lot at stake

In this world
Luck is not given

We build our life
We produce a legacy
We control our thoughts
To create an identity

I will scream it from the mountains
Till it echoes deep in the seas below
They ask "what is the meaning of life?"
I say we make our own

Feel It All

We're always learning
Seeking knowledge
Always trying to figure out what's right
> What's real
> What's true

But it's an endless search
You can't get life "right"
> I mean no one has

There is no way to live forever
No one has come back from the dead
We have no way of knowing what's right
Every choice we make has a consequence
> A reaction

It all depends on what you're willing to endure

Stay up all night
Spend the money
Take the trip
Take a risk
Live on the edge
Confess your feelings
Speak up
Speak out
Cry when it hurts
Laugh till you cry

Don't take life too seriously,
No one makes it out alive anyway

Caught Speeding

We used to walk the streets
  Heads down
  Avoiding eye contact
Maybe you didn't even walk
We'd sit inside
Looking out the window
Wishing things were different
  Wishing we had more time

We have nothing but time now

Many people can't go to work
Many forced to be at home
  Forced to spend time with family
How crazy is that
We have to be forced to be with family
When we are at work, we just want to go home
But now at home, we want to go to work
  We're never satisfied

At first, I was nervous about the lockdown
  Not being able to work
  Not seeing my support system
  Being alone with myself
  Getting sick
As we began to live it

I realized it is what I've been asking for all along
Yes, it's a tough time for lots of people
      Anxiety, depression, addiction, neglect
      Loneliness or unemployment
      It is tough for me too
But I know that we grow through struggles

I have more time to write
I can sit and talk with my parents
I can focus on my health
      Mental. Emotional. Physical.
I have the opportunity to come out stronger
Maybe not in the way you expected
      But in the way that you need

With a foot always on the gas
We've been pulled over
      "You're speeding"
      "You're missing it all"
      "Don't get through, go through"
      "Turn around and look at all you blew past"
We're always trying to get to what's next
But what's next is now
If you are speeding through
You'll miss it
      Don't blink
      Don't rush
      Look up

Reminiscing

Focusing only on the bad
And disregarding the good
Is toxic.

Don't let the good cancel out the bad
Because happiness doesn't and shouldn't hold more
value
      Than pain.

Show, Don't Tell

It's all about saying "I love you"
Without saying the words
It's about learning how to love them
     And then doing it.
The little things are the ones that matter
     Those are the ones people remember
     Those make someone stand out

The Shift

People use you
And once they have no use for you anymore
They'll kick you to the curb

I used to think
Real friends were the ones who
      Would reach out first
      Would check in unprompted
It created a simple measuring stick for me

Maturing is learning
You have to tell people what you need
      What you want
You can't expect them to read your mind
The ones who listen
      Then act
Are the real ones

Dear Younger Me

Don't give yourself away for free
Hold your heart close to the vest
If they don't ask, don't share
        They usually don't care

Say what you mean the first time
Say how you feel every time
        The people who make adjustments
        Are the ones that are listening

If they show you their true colors
But follow it with excuses
Trust that
Don't give them another chance to hurt you
        They'll take that chance
And get the impression their behavior is acceptable

Observe and take note of the little things
Remember who was with you in the shadows
Because it's easy to see and be seen
In the light

Quality Time

The best gifts a person could give
Are the ones you can't buy

I want to sit around a fire
       Chairs close together
       Telling stories
       Recalling memories
       And laughing till my belly hurts
I want to lay down together on a clear night
       A night where your breath creates a fog
       Snuggled with pillows and blankets
       Pointing out the constellations
       My eyes watering from the brisk air
I want a car full of people cruising down dark roads
       Lights outside of houses to guide the way
       Christmas music blaring from the speakers
       Snacking on decorated Christmas cookies
       And a magical Christmas morning
       Where mysterious gifts appear overnight
       Lights reflect from wall to wall
       The aroma of fresh coffee diffuses through the house
       With the slight chill you feel standing by the window
I want to lay in a hammock on a warm summer day
       Staring at the clouds
       Debating what shape they take

I want to dust off old board games
>   Or find a deck of cards for game night
>   A bowl of snacks in the middle of the floor
>   Plenty of drinks in the fridge
>   And you can feel the competition in the air
I want to sit in my beach chair
>   Soaking up the sun
>   Feet buried in the hot sand
>   A thick, salty mist spraying from the waves
I want to sit around the table with my family
>   And never get up
>   No one leaves, not for a second
I want to sit on a comfy sofa at night
>   Peppermint hot chocolate in hand
>   A blanket on my legs
>   Fireplace burning low
>   Watching snow flurries float down
I want the silence of a cold, snowy morning
>   Squinting at the glare of the snow
>   No one is awake yet
>   The snow remains untouched
>   Absorbing all sound
I want to dance in the rain
>   Like no one is watching
>   Like I'm the main character of a movie
>   And they just cued the downpour
I want to set up lawn chairs in the garage

During a summer storm
Thunder crashing
Lightning flashing
I want to travel the world and see new places
I want to be the only party in the movie theater
So we can sing as loud as we want
I want to feel someone looking at me
With eyes that never wander
I want to hold someone and be held right back
Feeling time stop around me
I want someone to wipe my tears
I want to live in the moments where you know immediately
"I'll remember this for an eternity"

If you could box up any one of those things
Put a pretty bow on it
That would be what I ask for as a gift
People
Emotion
Moments
And most of all,
Time

Before the Buzzer

There's no way of knowing
What your future holds
Whether you'll struggle or strive
Whether you'll sink or swim
The clock is always ticking
        And it is never in your favor

Leaves will change their color
The ball eventually stops bouncing
Your pen may run out of ink
So don't hesitate to take your shot
Because another one may never come

Epilogue

The Well

I saw a well and walked up to it
Filled to the top with shimmering, clean water
It had some leaves floating on the surface
Anything big or heavy would sink to the bottom
like an anchor

There was a rusty, wooden bucket
Worn and old, but still in working condition
I lowered the bucket then pulled it back up
When it broke the surface
The cool water fell on me like a waterfall
I felt so refreshed and new
Eager for more so I filled it again
      And again
And with every bucketful
Came a new wave of emotion, calm, and adventure
I continued to dive deeper and deeper
Until my exhausted arms could no longer lift the
bucket

Finally, I put the books back on the shelf
Saved them for another refreshing day of reading

Acknowledgments

This collection of poems includes poetry from my very first poem to the current year of working on this project, spanning a total of 14 years of adolescence, emotions, life changes, and struggles. With that in mind, I have lots of people to thank for being on this journey with me. Right off the bat, I'd like to give the biggest thank you to my friends—my chosen family. Without them, this project would be collecting dust in the back of my desk drawer.

Thank you to Glove, Shea, and Carson for the peer pressure to overcome my fear of sharing my work, and in turn, my heart, with other people. I love you guys always.

Thank you Kammy Kasher for the many coffee dates, motivational sticky notes, accountability check-ins, and discussions about specific issues throughout the process. You were this project's first reader and I thank you for being its number one fan and loving it, especially when I didn't. You are one of the main reasons I was able to complete this with my sanity. Your heart is so big and I am so lucky to be held in a tiny part of it. I love you!

Thank you to Dodger and Pops for the unending support, from campfire readings to just being there to make life feel less heavy. You guys are my best friends and like brothers to me. Hate you sometimes, love you always!

Thank you to Stephen for always checking in, always asking what I am working on, always answering, and being a brother to me. Your creativity inspires me to always express myself and be myself.

Thank you to Kimberly "Georgie" Garcia for always encouraging me to keep writing and shooting down every single excuse I came up with. Love you work bestie!

Thank you to my sisters: Sydni Bickford, Stephanie Watts, and Kelsi Mahoney. You all were my first-ever poetry readers and my first-ever supporters. I love you guys! Go Rivals!

Thank you to my bestie Hannah [et al.] Calloway who was my accountability/writing partner throughout college. I love you and my sweet nephew!

Thank you to all of my friends not previously mentioned by name who supported me and inspired me along the way. You all make me better. Growing up, one of my summer camp counselors would tell us the same thing each year at our overnight campfires, and it stuck with me to this day (Shout out to El Oso for this). He said: "There are three things you should always remember to say to your family, 'Thank you,' 'I'm sorry," and 'I love you.'" I remember him explaining that this can be extended to all the people you love, and to make sure you tell them while they can hear it. This is my forever "thank you" for choosing me and being in my life. This is my forever "I'm sorry" if I hurt you, if we grew apart, or if we fell out. This is my forever "I love you." No matter how far apart we may drift, if we talk every day, or if we keep up with each other from a distance, I will always hold space for you; I will always love you, and I will always care about you.

I would like to give a giant thank you to my mentor, advisor, and friend, Dr. Kimberly Angle. She believed in me and my writing from the second she met me. She aided my writing process and supported my pursuit of creative writing even after college. Thank you for being a touchstone and an inspiration in my journey with writing; I want to be just like you when I grow up. Your unwavering encouragement has meant the world to me.

Thank you to Alyssa Pressler, owner of That's Novel Books in Charlotte, NC. I met Alyssa through a writing club that she hosts at her bookshop, a time for people to write whatever they feel like working on and have the opportunity to share, receive feedback, and ask questions about their work. I stumbled upon this for the first time during a period of my life where I was not writing and was struggling to find the motivation to jump back in. Having the space to work on writing around people who were going through a similar process made all the difference in the world. Alyssa, you made this project a possibility. Thank you!

I'd like to thank all of my English teachers throughout the years. As a current employee of the public school system, I feel like teachers are so important to the growth and development of the next generation, and I think it's important to remember where you came from. Thank you to: Ms.

Smercina, Ms. Bryant, Ms. Adams, Ms. Patterson, Ms. Gibson (Tennant to be Gibson when I was in her class), Ms. Bernier, Ms. Parker, Ms. Blaylock, Ms. Shelton, Ms. Paulson, Ms. Goodson, Ms. Johnson, Ms. Corrie Greene, Dr. Don King, Dr. Nate King, Ms. Callan White-Hinman, Dr. Anne Juckett, and Dr. Howell.

Thank you to Aaron Lelito for your input, encouragement, and support on this project in the final stages.

Thank you to Alan Hebel for a beautiful cover design and interior layout. Seeing my work and vision for this project come to life with your art and creativity is a dream come true.

Part of perfecting your craft as a writer is reading; studying other people's writing styles helps you learn what you like and vibe with. I'd like to list a few books and their authors for inspiring this project (and that I HIGHLY recommend):

- *Feel Your Way Through* by Kelsea Ballerini, for re-igniting my love of poetry and reminding me the goal of poetry is to express yourself and your feelings.

- *The Next Chapter* by Jana Kramer, for teaching me to chase joy and find the strength in continuing to move forward.

- *Grimoire Girl* by Hilary Burton Morgan, for encouraging me to find and celebrate the magic that lies within.

- *I'm Glad My Mom Died* by Jeannette McCurdy & *Friends, Lovers, and the Big Terrible Thing* by Matthew Perry, for showing that it is possible and worth the work to write the hard thing, even if it is difficult to do.

I'd like to thank my family. I know I will always have you guys in my corner to cheer me on, hold my hand, love me, and stand by me. I love you all so much. Everything I do, I do for you.

Finally, if you are holding this book in your hand, I'd like to thank you. Thank you for supporting me. Thank you for going on this emotional rollercoaster with me. Thank you for taking the time to read my story, hear me, and see me. At one point, these poems were mine, but now they are yours too. I hope you enjoyed them!

9 798999 526151 3